REREADING Tagore

REREADING Tagore

AMIYA DEV

PAPER MISSILE
NIYOGI BOOKS

Published by
NIYOGI BOOKS
Block D, Building No. 77,
Okhla Industrial Area, Phase-I,
New Delhi-110 020, INDIA
Tel: 91-11-26816301, 26818960
Email: niyogibooks@gmail.com
Website: www.niyogibooksindia.com

Editor: Mohua Mitra
Design: Shashi Bhushan Prasad

ISBN: 978-93-86906-30-4
Publication: 2018

Printed at: Niyogi Offset Pvt. Ltd., New Delhi, India

To
Tan Chung
and
Ranjit Kumar Dev Goswami
for the encouragement

Contents

Preface

This is a collection of essays written over the last ten years or so. The immediate incentive for most of them was the 150th birth celebration of Rabindranath Tagore. However, a couple more predated that, one being a conference paper devoted to the novel, and the other a book chapter in a volume on Nature and Culture. There is also a third that was originally meant for a political science conference, but later redone as part of a centennial homage. The dates appended to all these essays are either their publication or composition dates, for not every piece had come out in print. One bears two dates being those of presentation and publication. Publication details of those published are also appended to them.

Conceived independently the essays do not cohere into a whole. At the same time they have some repetitions. Besides, they are of most uneven length, two very long and two very short. The longest was an endowment lecture; the one next in length was also invited though not actually delivered. I take this opportunity to not only acknowledge, but also express my gratitude to my hosts as well as printers. Their generosity had given me encouragement.

Naturally this book is meant for those who do not read Bengali. That may explain why I have quoted so much from Tagore, and that too in my inept English (where available I have used more competent versions). I am no translator; even if I were one I would be mainly rendering foreign tongue into Bengali. But to translate into English and that again from Tagore, was a difficult proposition. That difficulty was multiplied when I was handling verse, especially songs, the bulk indeed of my endeavour here. I can only beg my reader's indulgence and ask forgiveness for whatever non-poetry I have produced.

Tagore's greatness and versatility can be surmised outwardly. But to be told that he was great and versatile and to have a taste of that greatness and versatility are two different things. Hence my call here: come, let us read as much Tagore as possible. I have named the book *Rereading Tagore*, for that is what I am doing. Hope I shall be pardoned for naming the book after an act of mine. It is not a blanket thrust of subjectivity on the objective phenomena of Tagore's writings. Writings are no doubt immanent, but they come to cognizance when a reader reads them. And surely a reader cannot turn *tabula rasa* at reading, for memories are no locker-happy baggage. Reading Tagore s/he may not only be reminded of others far and near, but also of Tagore himself, far and near. Indeed reading a Tagore text can be an exciting experience that way, one text leading to a number of others.

This is my rereading. If this turns out to be my reader's rereading too, then I shall be happy to learn a lesson in humility. Humility also binds me in debt to Himadri Banerjee, Nirmalkanti Bhattacharjee, Rimli Bhattacharya, Sourin

Bhattacharya, Moinak Biswas, Pranab Biswas, Probal Dasgupta, Uma Dasgupta, Amlan Datta, Arun Dey, Sankha Ghosh, Harjeet Singh Gill, Swapan Majumdar, and Mitra Mukherjee Parikh for their help during writing and after. I have a special debt to Subha Chakraborty Dasgupta for going through the manuscript and mending my lapses.

Amiya Dev
September 2017
Kolkata

My Tagore

What do I mean by 'my Tagore'? Is his being mine not being others' as well? Surely I do not mean that. But I may be focusing on an aspect of Tagore that others may not be. Or, it may be the other way round. For instance, there are those who take him for a bridge between civilisations. To them his idea of *visva* or the world is of crucial importance today, especially after Huntington's post-Cold War thesis of the 'Clash of Civilisations'. But among them are also those that take him for an apostle of Asia, whether or not in view of his disillusionment with western civilisation at the end of his life and concomitant hope of a Saviour from the East.

That he was an early critic of nationalism as the source of geopolitical arrogance as opposed to intercultural hospitality is highlighted by many. They have in mind both his angry and sad words to Poet Noguchi over Japan's aggression of China and his reservation about Indian nationalists. Tagore's own words on his 'political philosophy' apropos a book of that name in 1929 may provide an extra cue to the latter. The year 1929 was also when he had a political conversation with a Korean youth in Tokyo, rightly appended to his Bengali *Letters from*

Russia—conversation in which the latter spoke of the class struggle as the true road to mass liberation about which Tagore had his doubt, taking count of the cycle of violence it might entail. And wasn't he going to earn a bad name by deprecating the wasteful violence of the Bengal terrorists in 1934?

The full half-life he gave to Santiniketan to realise his holistic ideal of education is a subject of interest to not only historians and philosophers of education but also to environmentalists and lovers of nature. For it was here that he hailed the cycle of seasons and held such festivals as the laying of the plough and planting of saplings. And it was only a logical outcome of his vision that on the one hand, Santiniketan should find her companion in Sriniketan dedicated to rural reconstruction – a blossoming out of what he had earlier begun in the family estates in Eastern Bengal – and that on the other hand, Visva-Bharati (meaning 'world-scale learning') should be ushered to pursue the all-time motto '*yatra viśva bhavati ekanīḍam*' (where the world is one nest). Its various wings—siksha, vidya and finally, vinay complemented by kala and samgit (including natya that combined both nritta and nritya)—came to earn a character of their own, not to be found elsewhere. Not only did Tagore write or rewrite plays to be put up by students in festivals, but also choreographed dance dramas and often took them to places to raise funds for his institution. There is a painting by his nephew Abanindranath of old Tagore dancing as the Blind Baul in the play *Phalguni* welcoming spring. Yet it may be intriguing that when he began painting, first through his manuscript erasures and then through images arising out of those erasures, and eventually by means of a pallet – his last major field of creativity – he moved away from the Santiniketan style that had produced a number of painters across the country. But it shouldn't really intrigue us, for Santiniketan did not create Tagore, it was Tagore that had created Santiniketan.

Take Tagore's life, the private and the public: isn't it worth scaling? He has two autobiographies, one written past fifty, the other towards the end of his life. But both *My Reminiscences* (*Jibansmriti*) and *My Boyhood Days* (*Chelebela*) are fragmentary, maybe the former less than the latter, containing quite a bit of his *Lehrjahre* and evoking a parallel to Goethe's autobiography, *Aus meinem Leben*: *Dichtung und Wahrheit*. Besides he has those letters written to a niece from the family estates in East Bengal, rightly collected as *Chinnapatra* or Loose Leaves (the pun not overruled), for they are also in part diary entries, a veritable foliage of sensations. I remember a film made on it – actually a string of stills – by a Bangladeshi amateur with much soothing light on its river-run and riverbank locations; but there is an 'I' in these loose leaves that the biographer needs must trace out. Speaking of autobiographies, there is a brief third one put together after his death as *Atmaparichay* (Self Revealed) from reflections on his poetic self, along with a letter he had written in 1910 to the Assistant Editor of the *Bengalee* magazine, giving a few bare facts of his life. To this can be added the 'Autobiographical' *Talk* he gave in China during his visit there in 1924. And which biographer wouldn't look up his hundreds and hundreds of letters, to whoever had written to him and to whomever he had written? His correspondence with Gandhi is part of India's annals now, though surely not that alone but a great many other deeds, his raising of voice against the Bengal Partition, abjuration of the knighthood in reaction to Jallianwala Bagh, and protest against the Hijli firing among them, would probably include him among the 'makers of modern India'. At the same time the biographer would look into his travels, he being a most widely travelled Indian; and last but not least, his conversations with world personalities. He is also revealed in his son's or nieces' or a grandson's memoirs and in the accounts given by his literary and other successors of his person and personality. An elder to my generation used to say that one of our great losses in life was not seeing Rabindranath Tagore.

All this and more is prolegomena to 'my Tagore'. Now, how do *I* approach him? Amit Chaudhuri has recently brought out a collection of essays, *On Tagore*: *Reading the Poet Today*[1]. His approach is that of a writer. He writes in English, but he has read Tagore in the original. And his focus is on the poetry including songs along with their music (being a singer he has access to that). I am not a writer. My approach is as a reader, and though not as a connoisseur, let alone a practitioner, as a listener to his songs and a viewer of his paintings. I am what you may call the common recipient of Tagore's creative arts. Of course the bulk of this reception is to the written word, to how it attains its rhythm and makes metaphoric and metonymic tandem with everyday experience. I am not speaking of verse alone, but of prose as well, the whole variety of it. I am speaking of 'language' where silence and innuendo are as potent as voice, the oblique as effective as the direct. All this is old hash to the students of style, but having denied Tagore the modernist heights and seeing more pathetic fallacy than

1 Amit Chaudhuri, *On Tagore*: *Reading the Poet Today* (New Delhi: Penguin Viking, 2012).

synaesthesia in him, maybe a little too long, I have woken up to the power of his words. Better late than never.

I have elsewhere spoken at some length of Tagore's power of words. Here let me give two instances to begin with. The first sentence in the first *Letter from Russia*, written to his son, has three units (four words in the original): 'to Russia', 'finally', '[I] have arrived'. I draw your attention to the 'finally'. He could have simply said, 'To Russia [I] have arrived', instead he is saying, 'finally [I] have arrived'. The 'finally' may take us back to what he had been told about the USSR, especially by his grand-nephew Soumendranath Tagore; or even, by default, to the unhappiness caused during his visit to China by the Chinese Communist Party's opposition to the thrust of his *Talks* there (wasn't Lu Xun later happy about his visit to the Soviet Union?). He might also have in mind what the Korean youth had told him a year ago in Tokyo about the necessity of class struggle. Besides, he had been meaning to visit Russia, and had even once thought of taking the overland route from Korea where, however, he could not unfortunately cross over from Japan because of ill health. The 'finally' may also in part be looking forward to what he is going to reveal to his son in the very first letter, the hint being that the visit was fully worthy. If he hadn't come he might have been deprived of something worth seeing.

My second instance is from the play *Muktadhara*. It came as a thud to me the other evening as I was watching a production of the play by a troupe from Bangladesh. The words are roughly—'The world is replete with words; you plug out your ears on any side, your death shaft will come from there.'[2] They

2 The translation is throughout mine unless otherwise stated.

are spoken by Dhananjay Bairagi to his followers who have come with him to their rulers further upstream who had built a dam across the river thus depriving them of irrigation water for their farmlands downstream. They have come to claim their governor back, the Prince who had not only condoned their lapse of rent but helped them break open a blocked-up mountain pass jeopardising his own people's monopoly over the downstream people's produce of wool. The Bairagi's words can thus be put in context: it is a hostile air they have entered, an air charged with vengeance and power. The words are of a general import as well, as often are the words of a *baul*, riddling, but only apparently so, in fact a surer way to truth.

Now, here is an instance of something quite different, reflective prose of a poetic quality. He was speaking to his school on a Wednesday in 1909. The subject of his talk was 'Seeing'.

> So there it is, this light, coming day after day, in thrust after thrust. It has been coming for ages, every single day. This messenger of light is bringing a hope every day to flower-orchards, telling the buds that have just opened, 'You are not aware today, but you too will spread all your petals and fully bloom out in fragrance and beauty.' This messenger of light is giving its radiant blessings to paddy-fields and telling the paddy every day, 'You think your part is all done by this supple swaying in the wind and by your pleasant freshness giving visual joy to all around? But no, one day from the centre of your life will shoot forth a stalk and that will fill you up with corn.' Light brings the daily hope

> of blooming to the yet-to-bloom flower, of crops to the yet-to-fertilise paddy. Everyday this shining hope appears to flower-orchards and paddy-fields.
>
> But this daily light is not coming to flower-orchards and paddy-fields alone. It is this that is tearing off our veil of sleep every morning. Does it have no words to us too? Is not this light bringing us a hope every day, the hope whose fulfilment is lying blind in us like a bud, whose cornstalk has not yet raised its head from the centre of our life to the sky above?
>
> Light is only telling us one word every day, 'See.' That's all. 'Look once and see.' Nothing else.
>
> We open our eyes and see. But that seeing is only a bud of seeing, yet blind. In that seeing the heavenward stalk to bear the corn of seeing hasn't yet shot forth. The fully bloomed seeing hasn't yet happened; we haven't yet seen the abundant seeing.
>
> Yet, every morning light comes from far afar and says, 'See.'...

It is now history that when Gandhi broke his fast unto death at Pune's Yarveda Prison in 1932 Tagore sang his famous '*Jiban jakhan shukaaye jaay/ karunaadhaaraay esho*' (When life is all parched/come in a shower of mercy), song, particularly dear to Gandhi. Suppose we ask ourselves, why did Gandhi need this song? Did it give him some extra spiritual strength at this hour when he had been daring death for the cause of humanity? Surely it was far from a ritual. Perhaps this is a cue to the power of Tagore's songs, both word and melody. This is also perhaps a cue to why he often thought of songs, word as well as melody, as the height of his creativity. This one song (*Gaaner bhitar diye jakhan dekhi bhuban khaani*) may explain:

> When I look at the world through song
> I feel it, I know it then.
> Then in its signs of light the sky fills with love,
> then through all its dust the great Word is told.
> Then it leaves the world out and comes inside,
> then my heart flutters at the touch of its grass.
> Lines of form and ecstasy's flow then lose their bounds,
> and then I discover that all around are whispering to me.

Can we still doubt that his songs are his bridge to the world of senses and spirit, that his words are his search for truth; that his lines and colours in old age are expressions of what he held inside and plumbed around? In one of his poems (a song) in the middle of his life he has an unusual metaphor (*aami hridayete path ketechhi/sethaay charan pare/tomaar*): 'I have *laid a road* through my heart,/there falls the foot,/your foot falls there.' Isn't that the business of the poet, the maker of rhythms, to *lay a road* to catch a footfall?

2013 (in Rethinking Tagore, *eds. B.R. Ananthan and M.G. Hegde, Rani Chennama University, Belagavi, Karnataka)*

Power of Tagore's Words

Some three decades ago, while lying on a hospital bed late redeemed from a brush with death, I saw two successive dyings on the bed next to mine, of an elderly and a younger man–with the house staff trying desperately to resuscitate them–two lines of a Tagore song hummed through my mind, the same two lines each time. I hadn't fetched them, they came on their own. I had heard them before, indeed a number of times in funeral ceremonies and memorial services, but without really heeding them. They struck me now. Belonging to his great grandchildren's generation, with a closer access to his successors and a newer affiliation, I had probably taken him for granted. In other words the legacy might have been passive. Yet the lines were lying in wait to catch me unawares. If I were a singer and had been on the fringe of a circle specialising in his music, or even a musicologist with some knowledge of his melodies, I might have had an ostensible reason for such occurrence. But I was far from either. So what happened was nothing short of an epiphany. Not only did I realise the unplumbed depths of where I had him dwelling in me, but also the very power of his words.

By power I do not mean authority, but magic. Words can perform it in many ways. Tagore spoke of his earliest discovery of one such way in the very first page of his first autobiography. It was a narration of how during a first-book lesson he hit on rhyme, the simplest ever, of a pair of two two-lettered words, and how it went on reverberating in his mind. (The rhyme was not as such shown in the lesson, though its components were there; the rhyming could indeed be called his first creative spurt.) He recalled this again in an autobiographical talk he was giving in China in 1924: 'I remember the day in my childhood when, after the painful process of learning my Bengali alphabet, I unexpectedly came to the first simple combination of letters which gave me the words: "It rains, the leaves tremble (*jal pare, paataa nare*)." I was thrilled with the delight of the picture which these words suggested to me. The unmeaning fragments lost their individual isolation and my mind revelled in a unity of vision.'[1] However, what I had in mind while speaking of Tagore's power of words was not mere rhyme or rhythm, or any other adornment they may wear, but a thud-like quality, a hammer blow that wakes one up to a sudden truth. It is like Tobias finding an angel at his door. In one of Tagore's songs we have a trope as it were for such visitation: You came the night my doors were smashed by a storm, but I did not know; in the morning I saw you and was struck with wonder. It is this wonder that words can offer, be it 'defamiliarisation' or *vaikharī* to rhetoricians. Again, it is this wonder that the poet packs in between the lines and words, endowing a far sight to the audience and readers. The *kavi* is

1 *Talks in China,* in Sisir Kumar Das, ed. *The English Writings of Rabindranath Tagore*, Vol. 2 (New Delhi: Sahitya Akademi, 1996, rpt. 2004), p. 590.

a visionary not only because s/he *sees*, but also because s/he makes *others* see. There Tagore has few equals.

It is common knowledge that though rhyme and rhythm endear words to us and help us to hold them in memory, they are not indispensable to wondrous utterances. Besides, rhythm is as much the life-blood of prose as of verse, though in a subtler way. Whether or not we agree with Mallarmé that there is no prose but only verse – one kind less poetic than another – there is perhaps no denying that Tagore's prose is often less 'prosaic' than expected. Here is a text:

(1)
Father came back from the burning *ghat*.
The seven-year old son – bare-bodied, a golden charm around his neck –
was then at the window above the lane.
He can't himself tell what was going on in his mind.
The morning sun has just touched the top branch of the *nim* tree in the house across:
the green-mango vendor had come hawking into the lane and gone back.
Father took his son to lap; the boy asked, 'Where is mother?'
Father looked upward and murmured, 'In heaven.'

(2)
That night the father, overwrought with grief, keeps groaning in sleep.
A lantern flickers at the door, on the wall hang a pair of lizards.
At some point the boy comes to the threshold of the open terrace.

On all sides the darkened houses are like the demon kingdom's guards, sleeping at their posts.
His body naked, the boy has his eyes lifted at the sky.
Whomsoever it is, his desperate mind is asking, 'Where is the road to heaven?'
The sky gives no answer, only the stars hold the tears of dumb darkness.[2]

Who would not call it a prose poem, though it is marked a story included in a batch of late stories in Tagore's works? Yet, does its genre really matter? What matters is that it grips us. Not only does it grip us for the moment, it also leaves a trail in our mind. Whenever we shall think of death, this boy's 'question' may haunt us. I am not proposing a thematic axis, but this may take us back to the Chapter called 'Bereavements' in *My Reminiscences*, especially to the following words:

> I was day and night drawn to the unfathomable darkness that was manifest through this hole [made] in life. … As a sapling stifled by a dark wall tries with all its might to grow as erect as possible on its toe and thus transcend from darkness into light, so, when death put up a sudden wall of an 'Is not'-darkness around the mind, all heart kept all the time trying with every strain to come out into an 'Is'-light. … Yet during this unbearable sorrow a sudden breeze of joy now and then began to blow in my mind, at which I was myself surprised. The sad perception itself that life is not utterly unalterable and fixed lifted the load off

2 'Prashna' (Question), *Lipika*.

> the mind … With detachment I saw Life's picture on Death's huge canvas and realised that it was most enchanting.

This last sentence may take us ahead – such is the extent of Tagore's self-intertextuality – to 'Death's ripple-less canvas is hung on eternity's backdrop, and it is on that that Life's comedy is on its dance towards the final act.' This is from his last novel, *Char Adhyay* (Four Chapters) that came out in 1934. Of course the tone of these words is different, understandably so, being spoken by a political activist cum terrorist who has sacrificed his *svabhav* or inner nature to the nationalist cause, and being spoken to the woman he loves and has come to liquidate.

But 1934 was a long way from 1912 when he not only published *My Reminiscences* but also *Chinnapatra*. True, Tagore does not have a single all-comprehensive masterpiece like Dante's *Divina Commedia* or Goethe's *Faust*. But that doesn't disqualify him from being an immortal of their order, for he has a good many classics, *Chinnapatra* being one of them. The enchantment of life quoted above is here illustrated. I am especially thinking of the words he weaves around the gifts he had of elemental Nature while looking after the family estates in Eastern Bengal, often from a houseboat on River Padma and its tributaries – the sun rising and the sun setting and the sky bursting forth in countless stars, the same cycle of seasons ever in their unfaltering rhythm, the earth's whisper in every spot of grass and creeper – and alongside all this, the life of rural men and women in their everyday sorrows and happiness, simple yet not without hints of complexity. In fact this was the time when he wrote some of his best stories, not devoid of drama but abundantly lyrical. In a letter dated 5 September 1894 he calls his afternoons at Sajadpur the storyteller's afternoons. 'I remember, it was at such an hour sitting at this desk … I wrote the story *Postmaster*. …I was writing while the light and the breeze and the flutter in the branches around me were adding their words to it. There is little happiness in the world comparable to such happiness of composing something at one's own pleasure being utterly one with the surroundings.' Whether or not *Postmaster* has all evidence of this *oneness* hidden away, there is no denying the story's power, and hence there is no reason to doubt this *oneness* as a valid poetic principle. I wouldn't invoke the famous Goethe-Schiller binary of 'naïve' and 'the sentimental'; let Tagore thrive on his own words.

Chinnapatra is a treasure-house of images. Some of them found a place in his poetry and fiction written at the time, some awaited future absorption. One such letter is: 'The sand dunes of the island are stretched out infinitely to the horizon—there is no grass growing there, no trace of trees, no houses built, none at all. The emptiness of the sky or the emptiness of the sea is known to us; we have no more claims from it—but the emptiness of the earth seems to be most awfully empty … At this evening sunset there is nothing else on this sandy island, none at all, only I alone.' This was dated 28 November 1895. Twenty-one years later this seems to be metamorphosed into:

> It was infinitely bare and empty all round with no sign
> of any life. The waves of sand were as cruel as the sun,
> crouching the sentinels of the void.

> … Everything about the place seemed to have been wiped down clean to a primeval dry whiteness, like a big No, under one's feet, devoid of sound or motion, of the red of blood or the green of vegetation, the blue of the sky or the ochre of the earth … like the vast lipless smile of a skull, like some enormous dry tongue holding out one long petition of thirst to the unpitying and fiery sky.' (*Chaturanga* [Quartet], 'Sribilas')[3]

It is tempting to multiply such instances of image made flesh, of words woven at one remove from experience turning into a crystal to emit wider light. How else would the futility of a woman's love for a frenzied God-hungry man ('Damini's heart sank as she stood in the centre of this pale, limitless white, which refused to answer questions or hearken to calls.') come alive? Again, being refused, how else would her hurt burn ('The empty sand all around burned like the eyes of the tiger at night')? Indeed if Tagore did not have such power of words, this novel would have been a telling allegory all right of the mid-19th century Bengali gentry's ambivalence between reason and bhakti, but not an intense all-time human image carved on that background.

What words can do is perhaps more acutely illustrated by Gaffer's 'Silence, unbeliever!' in *The Post Office* (*Dakghar*) giving the play a sure lift to its intended symbolism. But I shall get to that in a later essay. Only let me record that in a production I saw, I suddenly realised that this was the most

3 This and subsequent quotations from *Chaturanga* are from Asok Mitra's translation (New Delhi: Sahitya Akademi, 1963), pp. 84, 85.

difficult line in the play to be convincingly communicated to the audience, even by a then doyen of the Bengali art theatre. How did Tagore himself deliver it playing Thakurda (Gaffer) in its production in September 1917 in Kolkata to an invited audience including Mahatma Gandhi? The opening lines of its companion piece *Raja* (*The King of the Dark Chamber*) are perhaps no less potent: 'Light, where is light? Will never a lamp be lit in this chamber?'[4] But coming from a still disbeliever (Queen Sudarshana) and addressed to a firm believer (the Queen's chambermaid Surangama), they do not pose a problem in authenticity. In fact, the Queen's thirst for light is quite believable. The play is as it were an extended metaphor of that thirst – the fire set by the fake king and the war lodged by the rival kings, both aimed at the most visible Queen of the invisible King – and ends on that thirst finally overcoming itself and light dawning. Symbolism apart, the play is also a comment on the spirit of demos, one of its theme songs being 'We are all king in our King's kingdom', the lead to which is given by a Grandfather figure, ever in people's company, but unlike them, never in doubt about the King's existence. In addition, he often speaks in riddles, reminding us of Dhananjay Bairagi whom we mentioned above, who first appears in a play older than *Raja* by one year but takes fuller shape in *Muktadhara*. We shall have more on him in a short essay below on *Muktadhara*. One of the things we shall hint there is Dhananjay's probable overlap with Gandhi. To be sure, Tagore was no political activist of Gandhi's order, but he

4 Trans. Buddhadeva Bose, in Sankha Ghosh et al., eds. *Buddhadeva Basur Prabandhasamagra* (Collected Essays of Buddhadeva Bose), Vol. 3 (Kolkata: Paschimbanga Bangla Akademi, 2010), p. 449.

did have the vision of Dhananjay's truth which he put to life through words. Words were his main measure of action. One of his patriotic songs sees the hallowed motherland as part of the earth mother and mother earth, not a very common feeling with nationalists. At least twice he incurred his compatriots' displeasure, once by writing *Ghare-Baire* (*The Home and the World*) that did not approve of nationalist excesses, and again by writing *Char Adhyay* (Four Chapters) where he saw the futility of *svadeshi* terror and its human waste.

Perhaps taking his cue from William Empson's *Seven Types of Ambiguity* (1963), Buddhadeva Bose, a successor to Tagore, spoke of seven stairs in Tagore's poetry. The lowest is one where he is mainly a versifier, no matter how dexterous, and telling a tale that we may not else read in prose for having too simple a reversal and too obvious pathos. Yet not all such verse tales are so trite, for instance (for handy translations I am referring to William Radice's) 'A Half-acre of Land' ('Dui Bigha Jami') or 'Snatched by the Gods' ('Devatar Gras'), the former regaining a relevance in the recent land-grabbing by industry, the latter signifying the ultimate human values against blind belief (possibly not far from his first major play *Bisarjan* [*Sacrifice*] dealing with the inhumanity that goes in the name of religion). That some of the crucial lines of both poems flit across some six and a half decades of my memory, is not testimony alone of Tagore's sovereign status then in Bengali letters, but also of the very power of his words. And that he had this power even in his inferior poetry is not saying little. I am more and more convinced that a true account of his genius would also be an account of his experiments with words, no less in import than Gandhi's experiments with truth. What was truth to Gandhi were words to Tagore. Words gave him his truth while truth gave Gandhi his words. Such perhaps was the distinction between the Poet and the Mahatma, one complementing the other.

Buddhadeva Bose's specimen for the second 'stair' is still a verse tale, but better written and of a more intense human interest. It depicts a Buddhist monk's refusal to a beautiful courtesan's advances and his eventual 'tryst' ('abhisar', the poem's title) to her when she is thrown out of the city walls, her now-ugly body covered with a virulent attack of small pox. 'Harsh light hits those merciful eyes' is the description of the proud woman's stumbling into the sleeping monk on *her* tryst somewhere on the first occasion—a potent cluster of words. One would remember a companion Buddhist piece, written in the same measure, called *Pujarini* (Worshipper), a poem of greater import showing Buddhist martyrdom in Hindu India. It was this poem that was later cast into the play *Natir Puja* (Court Dancer's Worship) that unfolded the martyrdom in a number of concomitant themes, violence (one of its songs was 'World delirious with hatred') and fear being prime among them. At the same time the play rings with '*Buddhaṁ śaraṇaṁ gacchāmi / dhammaṁ śaraṇaṁ gacchāmi / saṁghaṁ śaraṇaṁ gacchāmi'*—words to summon strength of mind but not necessarily to hope for a telos. The play also rings with the word *kshama* ('*Buddho khamatu taṁ mama'*) that runs as a kind of leitmotiv. The court dancer's apparent irreverence under duress by way of a dance at Buddha's altar is also metamorphosed into a paean to 'kshama'. (One may be reminded of a *Gitanjali* poem here that begins with the words: 'With mercy my life / has to be washed, / how else can I touch / your feet?') It is well-nigh impossible to translate her song, but here is a paraphrase of the first movement: 'Forgive me, Lord, I bow to you, and invoke you, while dance stirs up my heart, limbs throb in praise of you, rhythm gathers, to left, to right, to give me a new life. I worship you today in my body's gestures, in my song.' Indeed, all we are entitled to after being a party to her death at Buddha's altar is to beg forgiveness.

The prologue between Bhikshu Upali and the court dancer confirming her purity to offer alms, may take us to another play based on Buddhist material called *Chandalika*, where Buddha's disciple Ananda confirms an untouchable girl's purity to offer him a drink of water. That brings about a complete change in her donning her a new idiom, a sense of self-respect. The words 'give me a drink of water' keep ringing in her as the groundswell of her *vita nuova*. It causes pain, but it also begs mercy, *kshama*. In fact *kshama* is the final theme of yet another text based on Buddhist material, the dance drama *Shyama* that goes back to the musical play *Parishodh*, going further back to the verse tale 'Parishodh', written within a few days of 'Pujarini' and 'Abhisar'. The last number of *Shyama* gyrates round the word *kshama*. It is sung by the male lead that could not pardon his love, the female lead, on finding out the price she had paid for their union. (She had sacrificed her unrequited young lover to substitute him, the stranger Bajrasen, the chance victim of a theft from the royal burse and sentenced to death.) Once again, I can only try a paraphrase of a rich text. She had begged *him* mercy, for the sin she had committed was against God and she would await God's scurge, but *he* could forgive her. Yet in spite of all his love, he could not. That was the human predicament. Hence his words:

> Forgive my not forgiving her,
> O Lord, you refuge of sinners.
> Love is not strong before remorse and shame—
> O Lord, you refuge of sinners,
> forgive me my lowliness.
> My lover I failed to clasp to bosom,
> it is love I have killed,
> to punish the sinner it is sin
> I have invoked.
> I know you will forgive her, Lord,
> weighed down with her sin
> she has sought your feet.
> But you will not forgive
> my not forgiving,
> O Lord, you refuge of sinners.

Of the seven 'stairs' identified by Buddhadeva Bose in Tagore's poetry, the third is illustrated by a descriptive poem dealing with the rainy season, 'New Rain' ('Nababarsha'). Not only is it rich in images, but also in sound, giving readers a special pleasure in reading it aloud to themselves. But perhaps it does not take them anywhere beyond, as many others of his descriptive or season poems do. One of these others is 'Barshasesh' (End of Year) written on the last day of the year 1305 by the Bengali calendar (middle of April 1899) picking up a powerful storm, come as if to end all traces of the old and usher in the new. In fact the power of the storm seems to be transmitted to some of its consonant clusters. It is often compared to Shelley's *Ode to the West Wind*, but surely as a peer. However, the first four lines of the last stanza contain a calm that may remind us of the last movement of Beethoven's Sixth Symphony: 'Still in new-sprouting cane-clumps falls the rain, / without rest; / on cloud's inner path from one darkness to another, / passed the day.' The rich cadence of their Bengali original constituted the very essence of poetry to Sudhindranath Datta, another successor to Tagore. Of course 'New Rain' could conjure up his whole host of songs on the rainy season, some of which are surely of the highest 'stair' in Buddhadeva Bose's scheme. This one for example ('*saghana gahana raatri, jharichhe sraabanadhaaraa*'):

> A dense and deep night in Sraban, rains pouring—
> an eyeless night with no warmth of companions.
> Listless I gaze on, at nowhere,
> where the pining woman's tear has been snatched away
>   by a star.
> The soft murmur of rain on fig-tree branches
> fill up the night's sleepless silence.
> From some magic land a shadow-boat
> sails out to dream-waters
> without shores.

For the fourth 'stair' Buddhadeva Bose has chosen a longish poem called 'Basundhara' (Earth) in rhymed run-on lines, thus in a way adding to his predecessor, Michael Madhusudan Dutt's *amitrakshar* or blank verse. It is representative of Tagore's love of Earth, expansive but felt in every pore of his self and is perhaps the ultimate source of his internationalism, so often seen in his worldwide travels. Its style is neither narrative nor descriptive, nor evocative either as in the case of the next higher 'stairs', but confessional or egotistic with every touch of sublimity. Buddhadeva Bose is now ready for poems like 'Sonar Tari' (The Golden Boat) where words and meaning are perfectly matched and where, as 'Sonar Tari's' complementary piece 'Niruddesh Jatra' (The Aimless Voyage) shows, some alchemy is often at work to accomplish it. 'Day's pyre in burning flames', 'waters glistening like liquid fire', 'the very rim of the sky in smelter', 'seething doubt this dark-blue water', 'an infinite weeping floating over the whole world'—are synaesthetic instances that may give us a fragmented idea of this alchemy. This is also seen in many another poem, for example, in a poem on Death that ends on: 'I shall go where your boat's moored, / O Death, my darling Death, / where wind blows from far afar / taking darkness' trail …' and finally, 'In a tranquil heart I shall cross / the purple waters of deepest rains, / O Death, my darling Death.' There is a sense of mystery about 'the purple waters of deepest rains' ('*mahaabarashaar raangaa jal*'), or for that matter, about 'wind blow[ing] from far afar / taking darkness' trail' ('*akul haite baayu bay / kari aandhaarer anusaran*'). This is proof that words can also surpass their role as ready signifiers. Indeed they may refuse to be emptied after performing their act of signification. That act too may be done at multiple levels.

For the sixth and the seventh 'stairs' we are referred to 'Svapna' (A Dream) and 'Anabashyak' (Needless) respectively. 'Svapna' is a dream within a dream, for Kālidāsa's Ujjayini where the present dreaming is located is itself dreamlike, with certain signs from *Meghadūta* set off, especially those around the Yakshapriya, his beloved, as the poet's persona says, from another life. But that love too is his yearning, his love of love, much unlike that of Kālidāsa's Yaksha, as evidenced by his lack of memory and speech at the crucial moment of their meeting in the dream, and finally by a sudden blotting out of the very scene and darkness and silence taking over. If this poem is Tagore's homage to Kālidāsa, like that other poem called 'Meghadūta' and those essays, 'Kumārasambhava o (and) Śakuntalā' and 'Śakuntalā', then it is a successor's homage who is conscious of his difference from the great predecessor. The duality of tradition and modernity that has caused such tension in many cultures is perhaps successfully resolved in Tagore: you do not abjure, nor do you idolise. While 'Svapna' grows out of a sense of irretrievability, 'Anabashyak' is built around a sense of futility. It is a dark poem, like some others in the book it comes from (*Kheya* [Crossing]), to justify perhaps the light that floods the bulk of the poems that follow, in *Gitanjali*, *Gitimalya* and *Gitali*. There is a hunger in this poem for light that is denied, the superfluity of that denial being succinctly held in the refrain, 'akaarane' (uselessly). The agency of this superfluity is given to a young girl who carries a lamp which, in spite of the interlocutor's entreaty, she sets adrift a stream in the evening, hangs as a sky-lamp in the dark, and finally in the black night, lets it burn among millions of stars in the sky. Such unconcern would perhaps make sense to Einstein when some twenty-five years later he and Tagore held a dialogue on the nature of reality. To be sure it was not Tagore's everyday thought, yet he came back to it in the last days of his life when his words became characteristically stark. His very last poem, dictated a few days before his death, reads (*'tomaar srishtir path rekhechho aakirna kari'*):

You have covered the path of your creation
in a mesh of varied wiles,
Guileful One.
Deftly you have set a snare of false beliefs
in artless lives.
With your deception
you have set the great man on trial
taking from him the secrecy of night.
Your star lights for him
the translucent path of his heart,
illumined by a simple faith.
Though tortuous outside
it is straight within,
and there is his pride.
Though men call him futile,
in the depth of his heart he finds truth
washed clean by the inner light.
Nothing can deprive him;
he carries to his treasure-house
his last reward.
He who could easily bear your wile,
receives from you the right
to everlasting peace.[5]

5 Trans. Amiya Chakravarty, in *A Tagore Reader*, ed. Amiya Chakravarty (Boston: Beacon Press, 1966), p. 373.

Obviously these seven 'stairs' are only one way of seeing Tagore's power of words, from the foothills as it were of Bengali verse to the highest snow peak. Perhaps a similar exercise can be done with his prose as well. From where he had begun under the shadow of his predecessor, Bankim Chandra Chatterji, to where he gave it over to his successors, is indeed a matter of wonder—several generations seem to have been compounded into one. And the net that prose has cast into the future! Do we know that when we write a sentence today or a paragraph, we are unwittingly following his deeply trenched footsteps? Our Bengali would just not have existed without his Bengali. When Buddhadeva Bose called him a 'phenomenon'[6] he was not exaggerating. Nor was Sudhindranath Datta when he said: 'For us, however, he remains the supreme man of letters: in forging our current speech, he remodelled our culture too; and when we meet sceptics, let us remember that reality remains in propositions.'[7]

To speak of the power of words is not to give priority to style at the expense of matter, for matter and style are so entwined that matterless style is as hollow as styleless matter uncouth. A writer writes and it may often be that his feelings and thoughts keep taking shape during the act. A certain turn of phrase may bring in an illumination that he hadn't seen before. Buddha's 'ihāsane śuṣyatu me śarīraṁ / tvagasthimaṁsaṁ pralayañca yātu / aprāpya bodhiṁ bahukalpadurlabhaṁ /

6 Buddhadeva Bose, *An Acre of Green Grass: A Review of Modern Bengali Literature,* rpt. (Papyrus: Kolkata, 1997), p.13

7 Sudhindranath Datta, 'Tagore as a Lyric Poet', *The World of Twilight* (Bombay/Calcutta/Madras: Oxford University Press, 1970), p. 261.

naivāsanāt kāyametat caliṣyati'[8] is the ultimate pledge of all sadhana. In his own way the writer too has a pledge: until words find him his feelings and thoughts and give shape to them he cannot give up. And of all writers Tagore was one of the greatest, and the most prolific—words went on revealing their rhythms and illuminations to him, all the time, for all the time he was coaxing them, playing with them, making them yield him their treasure. No wonder he wrote almost all possible genres in his language, nonsense and humour certainly, even 'firefly'-like sparks, epigrams, and a first book—a classic of its kind—let alone those weightier ones, absolute proof of his acclaimed versatility. Besides, wasn't it words that through their crossing-outs and rhythmic erasures yielded him diverse forms, eventually realising his dream of a visual artist? Perhaps the painter Tagore is the other name of the writer Tagore.

2011 (in Tagore and China, *eds. Tan Chung, Amiya Dev, Wang Bangwei, Wei Liming [New Delhi: Sage Publications India Pvt. Ltd.])*

8 *Lalitavistara*: 'Let my body dry up on this seat; skin, bones and flesh perish: until the enlightenment that is rarely found in eons, comes, let my body not move from this seat.'

A Word on 'The Post Office'

I had not seen Kanhailal's famous production of *The Post Office* (*Dakghar*) before. This May I saw it and realised how close we could be to Tagore even in physical theatre. Laid out in four stages – in existence, exile, hope, and dream – Amal came alive unparalleled. And sixty-past Savitri playing him was proof that Amal was truly the other name of Being, *A-mal*, un-impure. Since seeing Kanhailal the play had been haunting me. I remembered my boyhood acting in Amal's role in a provincial town on a makeshift board, with words like 'Panchmuda Hills' and 'Shamli River' choking my voice. Who knows what I had understood the play to be then! But do I have a much clearer understanding now? Of course this business of utter clarity is not always a happy proposition, though one may like to know on what wave one is rolling. Seeing or hearing is the work and responsibility of the senses. But absolute measuring up of the mind moved by the senses can only possibly take place in a land of lifeless cards. In 1921 Tagore saw a German production of *The Post Office* in Berlin. He liked it though it was far from his conception. He wrote to C.F. Andrews about it giving him an idea of his original thrust. Amal's world is not the world of

Madhav, the Physician and of course, of the Headman. Amal is restless and thirsts for the faraway: hence his confinement—he is 'ill' in view of a pragmatic world alone. There is thus an ambiguity in his death, what in one sense is end may in another sense be awakening. That its production in 1917 at Jorasanko bore this out is witnessed by that famous photograph of the last scene with Tagore standing with folded hands, as if for an epiphany. That its production planned as late as 1939 at Santiniketan was not going to be any different—production that didn't finally come through—is proved by the fact that one of the new songs to be added to it was the lately composed 'Ocean of peace ahead' ('*samukhe saanti paaraabaar*'). It is indeed not hard to see that the mere death of a boy is not its subject, that there is a deeper meaning to it. And that has been strengthened by the presence of a Post Office in the background that may bring the boy a letter from the King. At least the play doesn't have a negative bearing. The muscle given it by the words 'Silence, unbeliever!' towards its end is proof of that. (The Bengali original adds more by repeating the behest in 'Speak no words.')!'

Perhaps the Grandfather is not saying these words to Madhav alone but to those spectators too who are caught in reason's meshes, those who are only satisfied with the visible and the audible in the *mise-en-scène* and have no curiosity besides. But what happens in the last scene anyway? The malicious Headman has brought a blank sheet of paper and to teach Madhav a lesson who he thinks is audaciously ambitious, is faking it to be the long-awaited letter from the King saying that he is soon coming to Amal's house where he wishes to be treated to as simple a fare as puffed rice. The Headman's joke is first given a jolt by the Grandfather who says that he does see words written on that blank paper which say that the King is coming to see Amal with the State Physician. Does the Grandfather mean to console Amal or is he speaking out of 'faith'? Is he really a 'mad hatter' to throw reason into the air? Yet when it actually happens, that is, the King's Herald arrives with the State Physician and announces the King's imminent visit, how are we going to take it, as a coincidence with nothing to do with the Headman's joke? For can't he be coming on his own as part of his royal responsibility to heal a sick boy in his kingdom? But his Herald's mention of 'puffed rice' is too much for a coincidence. The issue of belief or lack of it may not thus be altogether irrelevant, though without much dent on Madhav or the Headman. Indeed the play seems to be laid on two levels. On one Amal's 'sleep' is death, on the other Amal's 'death' is awakening. Sudha's flower of remembrance may be a bridge between the two.

I once overheard a friendly argument between a poet and an agnostic over this play, the latter raising doubt about the order in which a *boy* dies for no fault of his, the former finding in his death a deeper sense. Indeed, how could Tagore fathom the meaning of life without coming to terms with so many young deaths in his family, of his wife, a daughter and especially, his youngest son in whom he might have had his own reflection? Rilke dedicated his *Sonnets to Orpheus* to Wera Ookama Knoop, a girl who died young of an incurable disease but who opened up to life more and more the closer she was getting to death. The death-devote Amal's thirst for life too was not to be beaten—he had the window when the door was denied him and when the window was shut, he had his spread of imagination while lying on bed and waiting for his letter from the King. This may help us understand why Janusz Korczak of the Warsaw Ghetto had his orphans play out *The Post Office* in July 1942 in apprehension of their imminent transportation to a gas chamber.

In André Gide's French translation the focus was on the King's letter (*Amal et la lettre du roi*) and in Zenobia Camprubi de Jiménez's Spanish translation, on the King's postman (*El Cartero del Rey*). Amal's waiting for the King's letter is complemented by his desire to be the King's postman bearing his letter to all, as does Badal (= rains) or Sarat (= early autumn). So, if the letter Amal is waiting for is tantamount to death, the letter he wants to bear is tantamount to life. The famous Spanish philosopher, José Ortega y Gasset who had written an open letter to Zenobia on her love of Tagore, wrote a second open letter apropos *El Cartero del Rey*. These words from about a hundred years ago are worth remembering, their crux being: We are all waiting for a letter from the King. More indeed, if by 'I' we do not mean our outward person alone reflected in our business or politics or social surge, but the deep and innermost core of our self; then what really have we done all our life except wait for that unearthly letter?

Taking the play as such as an *epiphanos* in disguise, what could be a better appreciation of it?

2011

'Muktadhara''s Relevance

A Tagore play that has a lot of relevance today is *Muktadhara* (*The Waterfall* in his own translation, both dated 1922). It is set in the open – in fact its original title was *Path* or 'Way' – on the road to Lord Bhairava's temple in a hilly country, with a quick shift of actors. The occasion is the completion of a dam, a marvel of engineering. People have come to celebrate it and felicitate its builder, Bibhuti, or have come out of curiosity in it or to bemoan their loss in its construction—especially a mother still waiting for her son not knowing that he has been washed away. They go in circles, with a chorus punctuating them, that of the Bhairava worshippers. There is also a choric song at one point in contrast as it were, in adulation of the Machine.

Not only does the dam's spire set up a challenge to that of the Bhairava temple, but it also cuts the water to an indomitable people downstream that have not been paying rent due to a severe drought. Prince Abhijit who has been their governor has condoned them their lapse of rent. He has been called back. He was the apple of everybody's eye. The King still loves him, but must now protect him from the displeasure of the kingdom – from his own people's wrath – for unbarring a pass in the hills, lifting the curb on those unruly people's commerce with the outside world and jeopardising the monopoly of the king's own people on the latter's wool.

As we noted above in a different context, those people too are here today in a group to claim Abhijit back though, being aware of the politics of the dam, *his* immediate concern is how to give them back their water. Their leader is a *baul* by the name of Dhananjay Bairagi, a character from an earlier play (*Prayashchitta* or Expiation, 1909), a rabble-rouser in the eye of authority, but in truth an awakener. Much of this awakening is carried out through songs whose words are often riddling, being a surer way to truth. His path is that of peaceful resistance which he teaches his followers. But as a true *hegemon* he would have them answer their own conscience and not his dictates. In him some see an incidental overlap with Gandhi. He keeps singing and goes to jail.

The play hinges on Abhijit, the Prince and yet not the prince for he had been a foundling by the waterfall. That knowledge has accorded him a special tie with that water whose flow he cannot see ceased. Not only has it been life to him but it has also been life to the people downstream. Every flow of water is life to *all*. No Bibhuti, however masterful an engineer, can deny it. Abhijit has come to know of a breach in the dam. Bibhuti is also aware of it, but he is secure in the knowledge that anyone who touches that breach will be swept away. A tragedy is in the offing. But it is a tragedy that will free the water. That is what '*mukta-dhara*' literally means: the freed current of water.

The three decades of the Narmada Bachao Andolan (NBA) may take us back to this play, written ninety-five years ago. In today's growing economies a special power is attached to the word 'development'. By all means must we have it, even by doing violence to both natural and human geography. The compulsion of capital is irresistible, and perhaps it has been proved by now that if anything is undying in human society it is that primitive accumulation. Not only does the state have its rhetoric of rationalisation but complicity—the recent history of Tagore's Bharatbarsha is littered with such complicity.

The *baul* Dhananjay Bairagi's entry song is symbolic of all nonviolent resistance. The opening words are ('*ami maarer saagar paari debo...*'): 'This thrashing sea I shall steer across with a storm on my trail / in this fear-routing boat of mine.' He doesn't run away from authority—he is ever there to be apprehended, but never ever to break. He is such stuff as morals are made of. Tagore is fond of such figures that go about in people's company and are yet ahead of them. It is them that people turn to when anything puzzles them: they can unveil a mystery. Besides they have such faith in an order of things beyond material power as makes them unassailable. Incarceration or torture cannot make a dent on their spirit. Indeed they have the makings of saints.

As we know, Tagore never produced *Muktadhara* himself. If he had, he would surely have acted in it. And it doesn't take much of a guess to say in which role he would have acted. Who would have spoken such riddles believably as the one that closes the play, to be followed only by the Bhairava worshippers' chorus? When the word is brought that 'the freed current had picked up his (Prince Abhijit's) wounded body in its mother's lap and carried it away', one of Dhananjay's followers says: 'But we came looking for him, aren't we going to get him then?' Dhananjay's reply to that is: 'Now you've got him forever.' That Dhananjay doesn't riddle for its own sake but for the sake of truth, is quite obvious in his firm answer to the King earlier in the play when he has been spotted as the rabble-rouser ('Of course, I do rouse them. I too am roused'):

> 'You shall not wriggle out by riddles. Answer straight: are you going to pay rent or not?'
> 'No, King, we shall not.'
> 'You won't pay? What audacity!'
> 'We can't pay what is not yours.'
> 'Not mine?'
> 'My surplus crop is yours, not my hunger's crop.'

Indeed the play is as much Dhananjay's as Abhijit's. If the Bhairava worshippers' invocation to Samkara – being variations on the same theme their two choric texts are merged at the end – is an attestation to the universal good, attained through such exemplary martyrdom as Abhijit's, then that perception is borne by Dhananjay. He is not only the *hegemon* but also the *choregos* of the tragedy.

2012 (in Mainstream Weekly, *ed. Sumit Chakravartty, Vol. L, No. 20, May 6*)

Ideal and Waste: 'Char Adhyay' Reread

We know that *Char Adhyay* (Four Chapters) was Tagore's second political novel foregrounding a love story. We also know that like *Ghare-Baire* (*The Home and the World*, 1916), the first, it fared ill with nationalists, and that a special reason for that had been his supposedly derogatory reference to Brahmabandhab Upadhyay in its Cue ('Abhas'). We further know that Tagore withdrew that Cue in the 2nd edition. All it had contained was a record of his earlier admiration for Brahmabandhab followed by an estrangement due to the latter's transformation into a rabid nationalist; and further, Brahmabandhab's sudden visit to him ending on a curious confession at parting: 'Rabibabu, I have utterly fallen,' leaving the impression that he had really come for that. However, my concern is not with *Char Adhyay*'s immediate reception, nor with the fuller implication of Brahmabandhab's confession, whether or not it had also hinted at a recent falling off his noble mission of adapting Catholicism to Vedanta. Had his brand of *svadeshi* come in the way of his truth, cherished with great ascetic fervour in the teeth of the dominant politics of contemporary Indian Christianity?

Nor is it my concern to test *Char Adhyay* out against the latter-day *svadeshi* of the early 1930s, branded 'terrorism', that claimed a good many young idealist lives. In a touching essay written in fifteen days of Pritilata Waddedar's heroic suicide after leading a successful attack on Chittagong's European Club and sustaining a wound herself, her preceptor 'Masterda' recalled her with great fondness, almost sentimentally, and bid her goodbye as he would bid goodbye to Goddess Durga on this day of her immersion. He also recalled the many others he had inspired to brave death or incarceration across the seas. How many mothers had he not bereaved of their children, what emptiness had he not brought to home after home! All for a great cause no doubt, yet was he right? Would he be forgiven? Iron-willed Surya Sen was pierced by doubt.[1] That Tagore, who had moved away from his *svadeshi* involvement during the Bengal Partition Movement before long, was pierced by more than doubt and had absolute disapproval of 'terrorist' violence leading to tragic waste, was once again proved by his reaction to the attempt on the Bengal Governor's life at Darjeeling in May 1934 causing a few youths' blighted future. But I am not going to look for its contemporary transcript in *Char Adhyay*. I shall be rereading *Char Adhyay* as a crucible of the time we have been living through.

Whoever reads *Char Adhyay* a second time will not miss its design as a virtual drama in four acts. Whatever gathers is mainly by means of dialogue. The attendant narration is sharp and subtle, except in the 'Prastavana', the prelude. The description too is sparse, as if only meant to lay the scene.

1 See Surya Sen, 'Bijayadashami', rptd. in *Bhashabandhan*, 4.11 (November 2006), pp. 5-7.

Also, the usual slow pace of a novel is missing along with the usual co-temporality of spaces. Novel readers will find more pleasure in *Ghare-Baire*—notwithstanding its triple perspectives—let alone *Gora* or *Jogajog*. Time-propelled it seems to be rushing, without a hint of space coming in the way of time. *Ghare-Baire*'s twin *Chaturanga* (1916) too is time-bound, but being a quartet it also carries four squares of space.

We remember Tagore's defence of it as a love story. Indeed to a large extent it is a love story, but that does not exhaust its scope. The three Ela-Atin dialogues that form the bulk of the novel have a clear crescendo, ending on love merging with death, a kind of *Liebestod.* But the 'star' that 'crosses' their love is the ideal to which they are bound, no less voluntarily than involuntarily. Ela is Indranath's recruit, sworn betrothed to the '*svadesh*'. But Ela is also Indranath's means of instilling the spirit of sacrifice in his boys and keeping their morale high, above all, of pulling Atin to the cause of '*svadesh*'. Over Ela and Atin's love is cast Indranath's shadow in the name of '*svadesh*'. Thus what turns out to be *Liebestod* is the eventual strategy of liquidation: Ela must go, for she has become vulnerable through her desperate love being taken advantage of by turncoat machination. That Ela must go at Atin's hand is Indranath at his most 'unattached': the distant whistle that closes the novel is the surrogate arrow cutting through the air. Tagore's critics of the time found such fiction unfounded on *svadeshi* ideals. Ela would probably swallow cyanide before spilling out the secrets. Ela surely would, but that is not the point. The point is: is the risk worth taking? Is she indispensable? Is anyone indispensable? Is there any room for love in the *svadeshi* underground? At the end of the third chapter, after Atin has been packed off to a safer hideout, beyond Ela's, or anyone else's knowledge, Indranath suddenly appears on the scene and scolds Ela for such submission to her eros and risking their safety, saying, 'If I could I would have straightaway killed you.' There is an impelling dehumanisation that Tagore is trying to trace, arising out of the underground's own logic. It is obvious that he is not making a transcript but mining out the truth.

Indranath has a dialogue in chapter one with his confidant cum assistant, Kanai Gupta, laying down his rationale of action. The crux of that rationale is *Gītā*, 2.47a, the famous '*karmaṇyevādhikāraste mā phaleṣu kadācana*'. Indranath does not quote the second line of the śloka that might have elaborated his cast of mind: '*mā karmaphalaheturbhūrmā te saṅg'stvakarmaṇi*' (Do not be the cause of action's fruits, nor have a desire for inaction). The '*mā*' of the '*mā phaleṣu kadācana*' can either be plainly negative or prohibitive. But there is no ambiguity about the '*mā*' of the second line: it is prohibitive. Now, whether as the mere interlocutor or as truly desirous of *svadeshi*'s success, Kanai Gupta does raise the issue of 'fruits':

> 'But I think you are overdoing your denial of purpose to this enterprise.'
> 'Not at all. I shan't do wrong, shan't go mad, shan't shed tears by calling my country 'mother' and 'goddess'; yet carry on my action—there lies my strength.'
> 'But how are you going to fight your enemy if you don't call him enemy and hate him?'

'It's like fighting a stone you stumble on, with unexcited intelligence.'

'But you are not sure of success.'

'No matter. But I won't do an insult to my inner self (*svabhav*)'.

Svabhav is a concept analogous to 'karma'. One 'acts' in consonance with one's s*vabhav*. By doing this 'karma' (*svadeshi*) Indranath is pursuing his *svabhav*. But can he deny that all else are doing that—Atin or Ela, for that matter? If not, then by pursuing his *svabhav* is he not doing violence to the others' *svabhav*, Atin's or Ela's? That seems to be an issue in *Char Adhyay*, in fact illustrated by Atin's realisation that he has killed his *svabhav*.

Apropos this, here is another excerpt:

'Do you love Atin?'

Ela kept quiet.

'If he ever causes us danger, will you be able to kill him?'

'It is so improbable for him that I may not mind saying yes.'

'In case it is probable?'

'In spite of what I say, do I really know myself?'

'You have to know. You have to prepare yourself every day for terrifying eventualities.'

'I am certain you were wrong in choosing me.'

'I am certain I was not.'

'Mastermashay, I beg you, please release Atin.'

'Who am I to release? He is caught in his own resolution. His conflict will never cease, his sensitivity will go on being hurt. Yet, every moment his self-respect will drag him on, till the end.'

'Do you never go wrong in judging human nature?'

'I do. There are many who have two strands in their nature (*svabhav*). These two strands are dissimilar. Yet both are true. Such persons too misunderstand themselves and go wrong.'

No one would doubt Indranath's perspicacity. Yet no one would also doubt his will to use Atin's *svabhav* to fulfil his own *svabhav*-ordained 'karma' to which alone he has the right, not to whose fruits.

'Svabhāva' appears in *Gītā*, 18, in śloka-s 41-44 where it is defined in terms of the 'karma's enjoined on the four 'varṇa's respectively, finally culminating in śloka-s 47 and 60. Let me quote 47 that sums up *Gītā*'s position on this concept: '*śreyān svadharmo viguṇaḥ paradharmāt svanuṣṭhitāt / svabhāvaniyataṁ karma kurvannāpnoti kilviṣam*' (even ill done *svadharma* is better than well done *paradharma*; no sin accrues in doing *svabhava*-ordained karma) (obviously echoing 3.35: '*śreyān … svanuṣṭhitāt / svadharme nidhanaṁ śreyaḥ paradharmo bhayāvahaḥ*' […; even dying in doing *svadharma* is good, *paradharma* is terrible]). Of course *Gītā*'s 'svabhāva' (= *svadharma*) is grounded on 'varṇāśrama', though in a society bereft of 'varṇāśrama' it may take on a wider meaning, the inner self or nature, calling, vocation. In speaking of Atin's *svabhav* apropos Arjuna's *svadharma* in *Mahābhārater Katha*[2] Buddhadeva Bose also recalls Thomas Mann's Hanno Buddenbrook and Tonio Kröger relinquishing their respective family's Bürger-'dharma' and instead pursuing their artistic 'talent'.

---

2 See Sujit Mukherjee trans., *The Book of Yudhisthir* (New Delhi: Sangam Books, 1986), p. 83.

Indranath is no ringmaster, but he is dedicated to a cause that cannot do without Ela and Atin. Indranath has all the personality to persuade them and win over any doubt that may be lurking in them, even if for the time being. There are moments when he seems to be a bit like *Gītā*'s Krishna to Ela and Atin's Arjuna. But the Kurukshetra he is conjuring up is far from the *dharmakshetra* it is to be. Can the cause attest 'dharma' or does it also have an '*a-dharma*' built into it? *Ghare-Baire* posits Nikhilesh against Sandip's *svadeshi*, no less a patriot but not carried away by the passion of the moment, a personification as it were of Tagore's *atmashakti*. To be sure, Indranath is no Sandip; he is too bright for that. Nor is he pitted against a Nikhilesh to prove him wrong. He is a revolutionary *per se*, of the underground variety, though not entirely functional without Kanai Gupta's pragmatic sense and feel for the terrain. As hinted above, not much happens in *Char Adhyay* except revolution eating up its own children. Of course in revolution's context such eating is routine. What matters if Ela is liquidated, and by Atin who too is ripe for liquidation? Is it not proof that revolution is greater than love, which so to speak is revolution's waste?

Not love alone, but humanity too can be revolution's waste. 'The lie that by killing a country's soul can its life be sustained is going round the world today in many places,' says Atin. Reading *Char Adhyay* is to a large extent listening to Atin and Ela's perceptions told one another. At one point Atin tells Ela how he has been pained to see noble-minded youths gradually succumbing to inhumanity, without regard to revolutionaries' self-respect. His last confession could have come from the 1970s:

> Look, I have fallen to the last limits (let us not source it back to Brahmabandhab Upadhyay).... The other day our band looted a lonely widow's home. Manmatha knew her by village connection; it was he who had sent word to us and led the way. She recognised him in spite of the mask he had on and said, 'Manu my son, how could you do this?' After that the band could not let the old woman live. It is through these hands of mine that that contaminated money meaning our loss of goodness has reached its target to fulfill our country's good. And with that money I broke my fast. Finally I am a branded thief, I have touched the stolen loot and partaken of it.

It could have come from more recent times as well. Yet, this is not vandalism, this is wiping away one human for a greater cause, an ideal. We may be straightaway reminded of Dostoyevsky's Raskolnikov who believed that killing one old woman for the good of a hundred youths was no 'crime'. And that was the beginning of his 'punishment'. The moot question is perhaps of ends and means: can means be utterly independent of ends? In other words, can good ends justify bad means, or more, can bad means not contaminate good ends? Of course, Gandhi would ask us to ever keep our conscience awake to guide our action, no matter what ideal we are cherishing and what utopia we are trying to establish.

I recall an evening at a Kolkata crematorium in 1970. We had come to cremate a famous elder. There was a wait. Suddenly, standing in the waiting hall I discovered scores of names written in red on the walls around with the oath that they would not be forgotten, hinting at possible political vindication. All are annals now, but could the ideal that took them away afford such a huge waste? They were not a faceless crowd, not numbers like Mahasweta Devi's 'thousand eighty-four', but persons, brothers and sisters and friends. Visiting the Cellular Jail some years later at Port Blair and standing respectfully before those glorious names inscribed on the central marble, the red splatter of the Kolkata crematorium flitted across my mind. When Sombhu Mitra staged *Char Adhyay* in 1951, what impelled him? Was he merely putting Tagore on the modern board, or also recording a reaction to the 1948 left politics? And in 1997, what motivated Kumar Shahani's film *Char Adhyay* (in Hindi) if not the tragic sacrifice of human love on the altar of 1930's 'terror' against the British, sacrifice so movingly come alive in a female body being tossed on a muddy beach and the screen fading out finally on that?

The world today is rent apart by 'terror' that is fast taking the proportions of a mushroom cloud, yet a 'terror' that has an ideal somewhere at the back. The idea of a 'clash of civilisations' is too biased for that. It is not 'mere anarchy let loose' either, but regular fallout of violence. Its waste is massive, not simply in its victims but in its own ever-increasing human instruments. The *fidayeen* cannot be a casual recruit, a volunteer without a choice, but a suicide answering an idealist call. We shudder at the double waste. A certain righteousness reigns over the ideal. One may be reminded of Thomas Mann's dialogue between the frenzied cleric Savonarola and the enlightened hero of the Italian Renaissance Lorenzo di Medici in *Fiorenza* (1906). One may also be reminded of Tagore's *Malini* (1896) where friends fall apart on religious grounds, fanaticism running high. But the proportions we are dealing with are infinitely higher today, threatening the very roots of civilisation.

In view of this enormous waste, what would Gandhi have done? Fast unto death? And Tagore? Write a sequel to *Char Adhyay*? There is likelihood though that Gandhi's fast unto death would be foiled by a human bomb. And Tagore's sequel would draw twice the critique. Yet, today's civil society that feels hemmed in on all sides would do better to go back to them again and again. No matter what difference they might have had on this or that issue, on one thing they fully agreed: the human spirit will survive all wasteful blindness.

2007 + 2011 (in Mainstream Weekly, *ed. Sumit Chakravartty, Vol. No. XLIX No. 15 [April 2])*

Rereading 'Jogajog'

'It is 7th Ashadh[1] today. Abinash Ghoshal's birthday. He has turned thirty-two. From early morning greeting telegrams have been coming, and bouquets.' Is this opening of *Jogajog* (Relations) innocuous, a mere cue, without a hint of happiness? I am raising the question; but I don't know the answer. For *Jogajog* ends on utter suffering, on a helplessness from a biological bondage and a crisis of being. What shape that crisis would take in the second part of the novel Tagore had in mind is hard to say. But at least Buddhadeva Bose who had heard its gist from Tagore himself some three months before his death (in fact he heard little, for he later confessed that all that while he was spellbound by Tagore's face and voice[2]) bore witness in the final chapter of his book *Sab Peyechir Deshe* (Land of Heart's Desire) brought out the same year, that if *Jogajog* had been completed it would have shown Kumudini's ultimate inability to accept social dictates in spite of utmost effort. Does that mean that she was going to follow the footsteps of Mrinal, the heroine of the short story 'Strir Patra' (Wife's Letter)?

1 7th Ashadh: about three fourths way into June

2 *Buddhadeva Basur Prabandhasamagra*, Vol. 3, *ed. cit.* p. 17.

That, in other words, Abinash's sole parent was Madhusudan? And that his thirty-second birthday's happiness is not unmixed with sorrow? Bearing Kumu's portion in his psyche does he not retain a part of his childhood antipathy to Madhusudan?

We can make many such conjectures; but we should first remember that set to write a novel on 'Three Generations' (*Tin Purush*) Tagore ended up writing a novel on 'Relations' (*Jogajog*). I am not speaking of the change of title alone, but of the change of focus as well. Besides, even though a second part was planned, I am not sure if the present novel is altogether unfinished. Tagore might have initially thought of three generations, but it is clear that he was not going to tell us the tale of Abinash here (if he had done that it might have veered to the contemporary *Sesher Kavita* ['Farewell, My Friend']); the tale he was going to tell us was that of Madhusudan-Kumudini or Kumudini-Madhusudan. Abinash turning thirty-two is causality by default.

Jogajog was once dear to us for its depiction of a class conflict. On the one side is the decaying feudal aristocracy, on the other the sky-high bourgeois arrogance. On the one side is refinement, on the other greedy grabbing. That Madhusudan is Bipradas's moneylender is as inevitable as Madhusudan's desire to marry Bipradas's sister. To Madhusudan what matters most is money, to Kumudini it is self-respect. There is a series of similar contrasts. It is a long time now that the feud between the Ghoshals and Chatterjees had begun—the tale of upper-caste Bengali Hindus of Nurnagar variety! Pride is the root of all. Thus came the fall of one house while the other house's yet-uncontested victory was up for eventual decay through excesses. A self-made man Madhusudan has retrieved the Ghoshal glory to the utmost. Indeed our dialectic-seeking mind was pleased that Tagore had been finally drawn to the science of history. At the same time our middle-class mentality was beginning to take sides. If we could smear Madhusudan with some villainy it would be easier to extend our sympathy to Kumudini. Yet Madhusudan perhaps was no less a loser. It is his tale too, not merely Kumudini's in *relation* to him, but also Madhusudan's in *relation* to Kumudini. In other words, there are conflicts underneath the ones we are familiar with which history cannot possibly resolve.

If Tagore had only written a short story on Kumudini-Madhusudan, it might have begun this way: 'When with great personal enterprise Madhusudan had fully won the favour of the goddess of wealth and desired to marry Kumudini from the very house of the Chatterjees that had once reduced his forebears, the Ghoshals, to beggars, Fate wore an invisible smile.' Did Madhusudan know what sort of a girl Kumu was? Only the horoscope was consulted. His self-confidence was as unbounded as his pride. He had sprayed his 'Madhu' name over all his possessions. He might have also thought of making Kumu forget her own name. He is the master of his riches; he is also the slave of his riches. In that master-slave device all are always being crushed. And he thought Kumu too was thus crushable. Sapphire is unlucky for him, so he forbade Kumu to wear the sapphire-set ring given her by her brother. Since everything in his house belongs to him, he doesn't think it to be improper, let alone stealing, to take that ring out of Kumu's handbag without her knowledge. He has the first right, not Kumu, over any letter or telegram Bipradas sends her. Kumu doesn't have anything of her own any more. She is a slave. The idea of marriage she came with didn't take long to break into pieces.

Yet Kumu's left eye had danced. When the marriage proposal had come, her belief-system since birth made her take that as the marriage god's dictum. Though she was raised by Bipradas, a liberal positivist, her mental world was different. Not only did gods and goddesses have a place there, they acted as guardians. This faith came naturally to her, without any outside incentive. And it could not be hurt from outside either. However much might Bipradas have asked her to look into the proposal carefully, she had already got her inner dictate: Madhusudan's age was no impediment—the incongruence of she being nineteen and he at least forty was only apparent. On the other hand, it was not in Bipradas's nature to force anyone—he might have been shocked by it, but if Kumu approved he couldn't dissuade her. All he could do was to ask her to look into it as carefully as possible. So could the marriage that took place through Madhusudan's stubbornness (a girl from the Chatterjee house), Kumu's belief (her destiny) and Bipradas's liberal tolerance, be a very happy one?

'Does a mother choose her son? She accepts her son. He may turn out to be a bad son or a good son. Husband is likewise. God doesn't sell wares from a shop. Who can judge fate?' It is thus that Kumu looks into her marriage proposal. And 'Bipradas has a great affection for Kumu; he avoids all argumentation lest she be hurt. Girls can be so easily tormented; their heart is bare on all sides. It is to bullies that society has provided whips, and no laws protect the sensitive backs of the unshielded.' Madhusudan, on the other hand? 'That there is an art of behaviour with your wife as well, had no room even in a corner of his calculating careful brain; as butterflies are superficial to tall trees, yet they have to tolerate their association, so did Madhusudan look upon his future wife.' With these three perspectives we begin the tale prior to the birth of Abinash. If they were independent of one another, then the tale might not have been so complicated, though nonetheless unhappy. But Kumu's belief began to be hit from the outset. Her submission made no mark in Madhusudan's 'calculating' mind. Again that 'calculating' mind began to be gradually distraught by this hitherto-unknown experience named 'Kumu'. Yet didn't the initial commotion that agitated Bipradas on looking at their wedding's cloth-knot ('In ancient history Timur and Genghis had raised innumerable men's skeleton columns. But if the life-and-death column set up by this knot between shawl and saree-end is measured, to which hell will its crown reach!') have a basis, except the modern mind's objection to Hindu marriage comprising the male-female inequality? A little later Moti's Mother (Madhusudan's brother Nabin's wife is known by her son's name) too would be seeing the picture of another frightful event in which a young virgin was to be sacrificed to an unfamiliar male's sexual hunger—'Standing at the mouth of the dark cave where an unknown animal is crouching with its sticky tongue out, Kumudini is calling upon her god.' Ahead is the bridal night.

This god of Kumu's is Gopal. It is him she calls. The tune that she hums from time to time is Mira's '*Mere Giridhara Gopala*, *aur nahi kohi*' (my Giridhar Gopal, and no one else). When the seven-year-old Moti, that is, Hablu stands by her, touching her, she is comforted by the feeling that in this alien place she has her Gopal's touch—'At the very moment of sorrow she called him; he came and told her, "Look, here I am to console you."' If she can awaken Mira in her, will she not be able to accept a rough 'other' like Madhusudan? But he only enhances her disgust. Yet, doesn't his sudden 'Barobou'[3] call to her startle her and bring back the memory of her parents' strained relation; perhaps also of her wife-abandoned suicidal father's last pathetic call '*Barobou*' to her hard-hearted mother?

Kumu is tradition-bound and believes in the figures from the past. In spite of the licenses her father took and of her mother's consequent refusal to accept him, her childhood memory of their conjugal relations is a happy one.

Was her marriage going to be a mirage? For even with his attraction towards her, Madhusudan's autocracy and moneylender's greed are not diminishing. He seemed resolved to erase Bipradas from Kumu's memory—so strong was his sense of authority over her. Yet he could not deny her aura over him—'There is only one way of binding Kumudini with strong ties to his life, and that is by making her bear his child. In that fancy is his consolation.' And getting a hint of that Kumu's disgust grows intense. At the same time she blames herself: why can't she 'give' herself? So she has no choice but build a cocoon around herself and having taken refuge inside, continue repeating to herself the spell-like incantation, '*Piteva putrasya sakheva sakhyuḥ / priyaḥ priyāyārhasi deva soḍhum*'

Why cannot Kumu and Madhusudan have their union, who is more to blame, who less, is a matter of judgement. But is there really any need for that? Madhusudan is hard, Madhusudan is rough, hence the habit of resistance in Kumu. But what is

3 Barobou: darling eldest wife

Kumu going to do when Madhusudan is soft, Madhusudan is begging? She feels bad that she can't still like him—there is no respite repeating her spell. And how is she going to deal with the fact that Madhusudan desires her, desires her intensely? Yet Madhusudan knows that he is not worthy of Kumu, that his riches do not touch Kumu, will never touch her, that Kumu is self-contained. But is his love, his desire false? We may take a second look into Chapter 37. What I would call '*sva-bhava*' and '*a-bhava*', having and not having, are beautifully orchestrated there. This is the night when the Abinash seed will in all probability be sown at last in the Kumu-body, the uncleanliness of which event will be manifest in the first paragraph of the following Chapter: 'Was the call she took to be divine fulfilled in this impurity, this violation of inner chastity? Was the kill waylaid to satisfy the deity's love for female sacrifice; the flesh of the body that has no mind in it be made his offering?' Let us recall some details from Chapter 37.

Reference Madhusudan: 'With the night getting deeper, the hungry animal from inside slowly comes out in the dark.'

Moti's Mother is concerned: 'Who will save this girl now from her husband's pleasure?'

Madhusudan's realisation: 'Seeing Kumu today Madhusudan clearly realises that Kumu hasn't come prepared; she is standing behind an invisible screen. But how beautiful! What radiant purity, what whiteness! As if on top of the lonely snow peak has appeared a flawless dawn.' Kumu speaks: '"Since I don't want to deceive you, I am asking you to give me a little time."'

The silence between the two of them: 'Reduced to nothing, like a bottomless pit. Time has its mouth opened wide.'

A little afterwards: 'Madhusudan heaved a deep sigh, and the room was startled as if out of meditation. He rose quickly from his seat and going up to Kumu said, "Barobou, is your mind made of stone?"'

Description: 'Kumudini was stifled in Madhusudan's embrace. But she didn't try to disengage. Madhusudan said in a choked voice, "No, I won't order you (Kumu had said, "I am your slave, you order me."), still, you come to me." So saying, he released Kumudini.'

Kumu's reply: 'She lowered her eyes and said, "If you order me my task becomes easy. I can't do anything on my own."'

Description: 'She was wearing a striped saree with a narrow border. The flowing black stripes were wound tightly around Kumudini's lissome body (we are seeing through Madhusudan's eyes), as if they were a jet of lines—not stationary, but ever on the move—a pair of black eyes were keeping an imprint of their restless motion going round and round her body, unable to stop.' Draupadi's saree? Description: 'On two sides are the two of them seated silently—the night seems unending—in between is an insurmountable hush. Finally at one moment concentrating all her energy Kumu came out of the bed and said, "Don't let me do wrong!"

Madhusudan said in a deep voice, "What do you want? Tell me what to do." He seems to be wrenching out even the very last words from her.

Kumu said, "Come to bed."

But is this victory?'

No, I am not writing a film-script, I am only trying to mark the waves in Chapter 37. The more Madhusudan fails to understand Kumu and yet tries to win her heart, the angrier he gets with Kumu. At the end of Chapter 39 it was even said that 'the two veins on Madhusudan's forehead swelled up. Not getting a reply from her he felt like beating her up.' On the other hand, Kumu's failure to love Madhusudan raises her sense of guilt. She is responsible for her failure. She had thought that a wife would naturally love her husband; now she sees that loving is the most difficult thing. She tries to explain her condition to Moti's Mother saying, '"I find nothing in myself. How can I serve him with such a bluff? Last night it occurred to me that I am like a bearing envelope; I had to be acquired by paying the fee, but once opened it would be found out that there is no letter inside."'

After all her initial sympathy Moti's Mother too could not understand this reluctance on Kumu's part, especially after the part played by Nabin in order to bend Madhusudan's mind to the 'goddess of his house'. 'It is indeed hard for women to realise that Kumu's natural distaste is entirely genuine, that this is not her pride, that in this matter she is fighting a hard battle with herself.' Regarding this late lack of sympathy on the part of Moti's Mother, Tagore refers to the traditional practice of binding the feet of Chinese women to restrict their size, which also partly constricted their minds. In remaining true to her ideal of truth and her inner being Kumu lost the sympathy of her only friend at the Ghoshal household since her arrival. Truth comes with a price.

There is a conversation between Kumu and Bipradas in Chapter 46 that claims our attention. I am quoting a portion of that:

'"Tell me, Dada[4], is my inability to look upon my husband pleasantly my sin?"

4 Dada : elder brother

"Lives of different people are affected differently … changing according to event and situation; fixing a general rule of good and bad with any finality may end up being a rule alone, but not *dharma*."

"Mirabai's life for instance. Because she found her true husband in her heart she could abandon her husband accorded to her by society; but do I have that noble right to leave the household?"

"Kumu, you have found your god with all your heart, haven't you?"

"I thought so once. But when the crisis came, I found my heart dried up; I have been trying so hard, but he is not turning into a truth for me. My greatest sorrow lies there."'

Of course this conversation takes place at Bipradas's house where Kumu is supposedly 'banished' for the time being. When by no means was Madhusudan able to erase her brother's image from her heart (we surely remember those words from Chapter 37: '"So without his permission you are not going to change and come to bed. Is that so? … Then let us send him a wire for permission—the night is getting on."'), he commanded her with vehemence: '"Go, go to them. You don't deserve being here. I did you a favour, you didn't realise its value. Now you will have to repent."' But not only has Kumu come, she has also decided not to go back. For the hunger Kumu has roused in him, Kumu knows Madhusudan has Shyamasundari to quench it. In fact, it crossed her mind once, 'Shyamasundari and Madhusudan are made of the same soil by the same potter.

... They possess a similar mentality; as if the same wind blows across both Shyamasundari's and Madhusudan's respective worlds.' Hence there is no secret about their liaison. Besides, whom should the Great Ghoshal be afraid of? Bipradas? Bipradas has a huge debt to pay him.

But when that scandal reaches Bipradas's ears, he takes it not merely as an insult to Kumu but as an insult to all women. The responsibility, he knows, lies with society. He used to be pained by the society-sanctioned duplicity of his father's relation with his mother. He knew his father loved his mother, but surely that love did not wash away his mother's dishonour. Bipradas is an idealist, he is not ready to condone this injustice in human relations—'"Since women have no other way but to bear it, they keep getting trampled upon. It is time they said, we shall not bear."' He wants Kumu to not go back to Madhusudan. Are we getting an indirect support to separate or divorce from Tagore, some three decades before the Hindu Code Bill? We remember that in an early essay on 'Hindu Marriage' ('Hindu Bibaha') in 1887 he did not, incidentally, follow the neo-traditionalists in speaking disparagingly of divorce as 'prevailing' in western societies, in consideration of the vastly different socio-cultural atmosphere that might induce such events there. In truth what reigns behind the concept of 'chastity' is power and it is that power that Bipradas is protesting against: '"In the world today a battle is raging in the air against such indeterminate power rooted in politics and religion."' Will we be wrong to think that Bipradas had Ibsen's *A Doll's House* in mind? The fact that Tagore knew Ibsen is apparent in *Char Adhyay* (Four Chapters, 1934). There is also a hint at Nora's desertion of home in a poem in *Shyamali* (The Green One) written in 1936: 'Some have said that the Bengali girl / has been advanced by the author / towards Ibsen's gospel of freedom.'

It is needless to say that such views will not be relished by Moti's Mother for whom nothing is greater than samsara to women—whether or not the wife loves the husband she must perform her duties as wife. Even though Kumu's heart cherishes freedom she is her mother's daughter: she values samsara, perhaps not as blindly as Moti's Mother does, but to a fair extent. And in that light she makes a distinction of man and woman. '"We are involved with human beings, but we also hold on to beliefs; we can by no means separate the two. … You know a lot, so your mind can be free; we believe a lot which fills up our life's vacancies."' Does this confession come back as a boomerang with the knowledge of her pregnancy? With whatever force she might have told Madhusudan that she wouldn't return to him, she would have to go back now. Her pregnancy to her 'is the worst injustice of fate'. 'There is something in Madhusudan that has not only hurt Kumu, but has also given her a sense of shame. It seems obscene to her. … With her own feeling of disgust Kumu has herself been fighting. … But she hadn't earlier realised the extent of her defeat.' On the other hand to Moti's Mother this is happy news: '"You are a daughter-in-law of the Ghoshals; would the guardian deity of that dynasty let you off so easily?"' Does Tagore suddenly close his novel by showing this defeat to that 'guardian deity' (we recall some readers' dissatisfaction with the ending of *Chokher Bali* [*Binodini*] once)? Or is he sowing a different seed in the soil of patriarchal or male-dominated married life? At least what we here hear from Kumu may lead us to that surmise. Kumu's words are of special import:

'"There is something which you may not like to sacrifice even for the sake of your son.… I am so made that they cannot give me any happiness. I too won't be able to make them happy. … Then why this catastrophe? I alone will bear the full brunt of this wrongdoing from society; they won't have the least mark of scandal. But I shall one day release them, I too shall find my release; I shall come back, you (Kumu is speaking to Bipradas) will bear witness. I can't be a lie and live among lies. I am their Barobou—but does it have any meaning if I am not Kumu?"'

Kumu versus Barobou—we may be reminded in this context: 'Why won't you give woman / the right to win her fate / O God'—from the poem 'Sabala' (Strong [as opposed to 'Weak' or *abala*, the traditional epithet to woman]) in *Mahua* (Mahua flower), written on 7 Bhadra 1335 BS (late August 1928). Which course would Tagore have Kumu take to attain her eventual freedom? We are told that the stage wizard Sisir Kumar Bhaduri's conjecture didn't quite please Tagore. We notice that apropos Kumu's pregnancy her imminent physical motherhood doesn't come into focus. Is it due to Kumu's allergy, or because of Tagore's probable preference for emotional motherhood to the physical? The fact that the heart's pull is stronger than the umbilical cord's has been best illustrated by *Gora*'s Anandamoyee.

But while thinking of Kumu's future, are we not going to think of Madhusudan's future at all? In spite of all his obtuseness, meanmindedness and revengefulness, he loved Kumu. Is he merely going to try to throw Bipradas into a gutter and do policing over Kumu? Doesn't the dual *israj* by brother and sister on the morning of Kumu's departure, remind us of Sakuntala's departure from Kanva's hermitage and create any vibration in the richly decorated carriage waiting downstairs? Does the novel have a sudden end in the midst of utter vacancy? Only the whimper of a dog bears witness to the tragedy?

The last installment of *Jogajog* was printed in *Bichitra* in Chaitra 1335 BS (March-April 1929). And it is in Chaitra 1335 BS that the last installment of *Sesher Kavita* came out in *Prabasi*. The two books also came out in the same year, 1336 BS. What a strange coincidence! Perhaps no two works are so contrary as *Jogajog* and *Sesher Kavita*. As if while writing *Jogajog* Tagore had at one point a desire to write its 'other'. And the people it presents are not at all like Kumudini-Madhusudan-Bipradas, seemingly a few decades ahead of them in time. In place too they have a difference. They haven't heard of Nurnagar or Rajabpur; beside Kolkata their geography contains a bit of 'Paschim', that is, northern western and western India, and England (Bilet), and for summer, the hills. Their social class is doubtless non-low, even non-middle. Ketaki turning into Ketty and back into Ketaki again doesn't make any social change. Will it be too fanciful to say that in *Sesher Kavita* and its kind Tagore is telling the tale of Abinash Ghoshal's time and place? It doesn't take much for the characters to be socially indifferent, as if society is a distant noise not needed to be heeded, or a congregation of their likes where the antagonist too provides pleasure. No 'peasant girl' is seen here who was being lured to an Assam tea estate by a 'tout', but who has escaped him and come back. Here there is no 'niggardly winter night of Kolkata, smudged in smoke and fog, with an unpleasant sky, and starlight like words from a croaked voice.' Compared to the Mira songs learnt from Bipradas which are Kumu's refuge or the *mantra*-like Sanskrit slokas, Amit's poems occasioned by Labonya's company are like jewels, sparkling. They are not born from the narrative's soil. In fact there is not much soil in such narratives, what predominates is the mind's play. In that respect the story 'Seshkatha' (Last Word) from the collection *Tinsangi* is most shining, no lesser to my mind than *Sesher Kavita* (the last poem that gives the novel its title).

I began this essay with a hint of happiness in the first four sentences of *Jogajog*. But I could not relate it to the end of the novel. Indeed I didn't try to do that, I tried to unpack the novel. While unpacking I came across living human beings and saw a regular spread of soil in it. It is rooted in time and place. I didn't ask why even after planning a second part Tagore didn't write it. For he hadn't abstained from writing; he was writing all the time. Maybe what he wrote was not in so many words the second part of *Jogajog*, but didn't he have Abinash in them? Suppose we think of an Abinash without Kumu and Madhusudan around him, but who inherits Madhusudan's money and Kumu's purity. But that legacy he carries around without any conflict between them. At his thirty-second birthday we have already put behind Kumudini's tale, put behind Madhusudan's tale. Without quoting the theory of genes, we may see him in Nabinmadhab's thirty-six from the story 'Seshkatha'. Achira's diary will end now.

Am I not saying in other words that *Jogajog* is Tagore's last big novel?

2011

'Gora'

Even being an ardent admirer of Tagore, the Kannada poet Kuvempu (K.V. Puttappa, 1904-94) would not call him a '*mahakavi*', for he had not borne the mind of an entire people like Vyāsa or Homer—he had been a '*sreshtha kavi*', a great poet of the highest order. Yet to one of Kuvempu's successors, the late lamented U. R. Ananthamurthy, Tagore's *Gora* was the most important Indian novel of our times. And I propose to read *Gora* as a virtual *mahakavya* in spite of Kuvempu's doubt. Of course at the back of my mind I am counting on the view that the novel is the modern form of epic. I do see in *Gora* the breadth and wholeness that Georg Lukács saw for instance in Balzac or Tolstoy or Thomas Mann. To be sure, those light-hearted lines from Tagore's book of poems *Kshanika* (The Flitting One),

> To plunge into writing
> an epic
> was in my mind too –
> but in the way came your bangles'
> jingle

> and my theme burst
> into a thousand songs.

were at best an excuse for not following his predecessors of epic fame in Bengali, Madhusudan, Hemchandra and Nabinchandra.

Tagore wrote *Gora* over four years. One envies those readers of the periodical *Prabasi* who first saw this many-storied house gradually come up. Indeed the house has many stories, and many doors and windows. One such door opens in Chapter 1 and its immediate resonance goes on for six chapters. Though the first paragraph of the first chapter is descriptive, it strikes a note of joy:

> In a morning in the month of Sraban, clouds have dispersed and Kolkata's sky has filled up with pure sunshine. In the streets there is no respite to carriages (presently we shall see its outcome in the novel's first event), the hawkers are shouting out their wares without stop; for those who will go to office, college and court, fish and vegetable baskets have arrived in their houses and in kitchens smoke is swirling up from the cooking fires—yet today this huge and cruel city of Kolkata, given as such to labour, has in its hundreds of streets and lanes a shower of golden light bearing a wondrous flow of youth.

The year, let us say, is 1881, and the locale is the neighbourhood named Hedua. That light has taken hold of an idle young man, Binoybhushan who is poised between his past and future. And though the snatch from the Lalan sung by the *baul* at the lane head is at the moment idle, it too is going to pick up a personal ring for him: '*In the cage this strange bird comes and goes, but how? / If I could catch it I would put a mind-clasp to its feet.*' The event takes place—a fashionable two-horse carriage hits a rented hackney carrying an old man and a young woman: the young man's heart wakes up.

Tagore did not begin by saying that Binoybhushan and Gourmohan are inseparable friends. Yet while describing Binoy's newly felt experience he let that friendship be manifest through the curiosity of the Brahmo boy from House No. 78, roused by Gora's portrait hanging on his wall. That the curiosity was quite strong becomes evident a few chapters later when, during Binoy's first visit to that house the boy Satish 'all on a sudden quite unexpectedly asks him, "Won't you bring your friend here one day?"'. The friendship becomes visible and audible in Chapters 2, 3 and 4; and with that the difference in their nature. Gora is overpowering, Binoy mild. Gora's strength is of his belief, Binoy's is of his affection—and perhaps it is his affection that makes him ever agree with Gora. At the end of Chapter 2 for once at least Gora admits, 'To all things I give excessively more stress than is necessary, and I don't realise how obtrusive it gets to others.' These words are followed by: 'Binoy comes close to Gora and affectionately holds his hand.' Probably Gora's strength is inherited by birth, though the science of genes was still not known. However, we do get a distant hint of the mystery shrouding Gora's birth in Chapter 3 when Anandamoyee tells him—'But you know by taking you to lap I gave up all rituals?' And 'hearing Anandamoyee's words today a certain shade of doubt has crossed Binoy's mind.'

Tagore had no intention of hiding the story of Gora's birth from his readers, they are told at the earliest opportunity. Chapters 5 and 6 are on Anandamoyee and Krishnadayal discussing Gora's growing faith in Hindu rituals and on whether or not he should be immediately disabused of them by being told of his antecedents, Anandamoyee so wishing, but Krishnadayal pleading deferment. In that context the narrator tells us how Gora has come to be such a staunch Hindu. What has really motivated him is his patriotism, an analogue of the debate between Rev. Hastie and Bankim that counters any humiliation from colonial quarters ('We shall not let our own land be in the foreigner's court like a convict and be tried by the foreigner's law.' … 'We do not want to put up a defence to anyone as to whether we are good or bad, civilised or uncivilised—only we want to feel hundred per cent that we are us.'). However much may Krishnadayal now retire in his shell of Hindu 'esoteric practices', his practical wisdom has not waned a bit and he expects the same from Gora. Anandamoyee is the very opposite. Without having given birth to Gora she is Gora's mother. Though forced to let Gora share his title Krishnadayal is not Gora's father. The fear of Anandamoyee's filial love compromising his worldly position is pushing him further into his esotericism.

As early as Chapter 4 we hear of Gora's India or Bharatbarsha. Binoy had asked him where lay his Bharatbarsha; Gora replied by putting his hand on his heart. Bharatbarsha lies in his consciousness. Bharatbarsha is the very Truth to him. He would like to call out to all and preach that Truth. He is a Hindu, but more than that he is Bharatbarsha's son. The resolution he takes in Chapter 6 to join the holy bath at Tribeni on the occasion of the solar eclipse, is due to his Bharatbarsha's pull to him: 'Gora has resolved to bathe at Tribeni, for many pilgrims will congregate there. He wants to be part of those people, dedicate himself to a mighty flow contained by his country, and in his heart feel one with the waves flooding his country's heart.' Binoy is left out of this resolution whose emotions are not stirred by any idealism. He only begs affection: his shelter is in Anandamoyee, and his newly awakened heart is pulled to the Brahmo family at House No. 78. But the Brahmo Samaj means an affront to Gora's Bharatbarsha. 'At every step has Binoy agreed to a good many bans put up by their group in the name of Bharatbarsha. A rebellion has sparked up in his mind today. It seems to him that Bharatbarsha is only an image of bans.' He rushing in Chapter 7 to share a meal out of Anandamoyee's plate, and at the same time drink water from her Christian maid Lachmia's hand (poison to Gora) is as it were ignoring that Bharatbarsha under the impact of his feelings. The novel is being rocked by this conflict between Gora and Binoy. But Gora too is going to appear in House No. 78—to inquire the well-being of Krishnadayal's friend from his iconoclastic youth, Paresh Bhattacharya—so is decided at the end of Chapter 6—though after his pilgrimage to Tribeni.

Narration goes ahead, but also goes back for reasons of causality. When at the outset of Chapter 10, whether it was to follow his father's behest or to put a curb on Binoy's new allegiance, Gora makes his appearance at House No. 78, 'his forehead bears an imprint of Ganga clay, he has a coarse dhoti on, a shirt tied across by strings, and a coarse shawl, and on feet Cuttack sandals with horns. He makes his arrival as personified protest against the present times.' This is Gora's 'battle outfit'. This battle is against the educated Indian who pushes out the half-educated and uneducated multitude. The steamer trip to Tribeni has opened his eyes. On one side were numerous awestruck beggar-like Indian men and women; on the other side was an English-educated Indian hankering for English company—as if two races. As if Tagore was writing an early draft of *Gitanjali* 108 ('Oh my poor country, the people you have humiliated' [not included in the English *Gitanjali*]). In this heart-rending difference between the high and the low he knows where his heart lies, but since he too is an educated Indian, his relation with the insensitive and self-satisfied Indians is that of battle. And the Brahmos he usually puts in the second category. What other than a haughty defiance does his Bharatbarsha tell him to dole out to this narrow community deviated from Bharatbarsha's ideals?

That was Binoy's first day too at House No. 78, but though unused to the Brahmo manners, his nature is compatible. Besides he is an individual, not like Gora his Bharatbarsha's verbal icon. We have already seen the 'modernity' of a Brahmo house's gathering at the tea table in *Naukadubi* (The Wreck), here it is fuller. This table's mistress Barodasundari to obliterate her village origins is practising Brahmoism with a vengeance. 'She is always concerned about the difference of what is Brahmo and what is un-Brahmo on earth. On seeing a Brahmo family eating seated on floor-mats she gave vent to her anxiety that Brahmo Samaj today is reverting to idol worship.' She is the proof of how fierce 'modernity' can get. There is only one other sectarian Brahmo in this novel, a daily guest in this house, Panubabu or Haran Chandra Nag whom Baroda, however, doesn't value much because he is a mere schoolmaster. The argument that takes place that day between Gora and Haran is caused by the latter's snobbery. Maybe this argument is still relevant as an instance of how disastrous an undigested 'modernity' can be. 'Is it to be said so casually that our people will never amount to anything?' 'Shouldn't we tell the truth?' '... If you had really known this to be true, then you wouldn't have said it so glibly and with such gusto. It was blurted out of your mouth because you knew it wasn't true. ... Falsehood is sinful, false denigration is more sinful, and few sins are like the false denigration of one's own people.' The anger that had been generated during his steamer trip to Tribeni is expressed here. Gora's *jihad* for Bharatbarsha is thus declared.

In fact, it is his Bharatbarsha that gradually pulls Sucharita to Gora, in spite of all his conservatism and arrogance. And this happens in spite of Binoy whose attraction to Sucharita has been causing vacillations to his friendship with Gora, and also in spite of her prospective marriage to Haran. We keep pace now with them—we sympathise with Binoy's fluctuating states of mind; we are fascinated by Gora's patriotism and love of people in his endless arguments; we are repelled by Haran's possessive attitude to Sucharita in the name of Brahmo Samaj. A new dimension is added to all this when Mahim puts up his proposal on his daughter Sashimukhi's marriage to Binoy. A vacillation sets in and goes on for about two-thirds of the narrative: the proposal floats in a limbo of 'yes' and 'no'. At the same time the actual picture of the Hindu society that Gora is so concerned with and would not like to reform from above, begins to be manifest. The uncouth press of the Tribeni pilgrims may, however, be overlooked on grounds of compassion, especially since there is a villain around—an English-educated English-loving Indian. As to Mahim, being Gora's elder brother and hence respected, his *bhadralok* attitude of compromise may not have to be counted. But how do we react to Nanda's death? A sprightly young man of twenty-two dying without a proper treatment ('at his illness' outset Nanda had requested his mother to send word to Gora—but she did not lest Gora came and insisted on getting a regular doctor to treat him'), by being roughly exorcised by a petty shaman? Foolishness? Yes, foolishness; but 'don't seek any consolation, Binoy, by thinking that putting this foolishness aside you can be outside it.' 'Gods, ghouls, owls, sneezing, Thursdays, inauspicious moments—there is no end to such fear—by what means would they know how to have a manly dealing with truth?' Yes, these are Gora's words (has Vivekananda dawned on him?). 'Binoy, I am telling you again and again, don't think it impossible even in your dreams that our country will one day be liberated, that she will not be wrapped up by ignorance forever, and the English will not be able to always drag her shackled to their trading boat.' These are words that Binoy only can be told even though he is relatively unexcitable. But he is conscious of his lack of excitement ('as we are unaware of our breathing so are these too to us'). Gora is not un-modern, but the modernity that breeds alienation is not his.

We are in Chapter 17 of the novel. We remember the novel began with a fashionable carriage hitting a hackney, though without revealing any social inequality. That is done in this chapter by another fashionable carriage. 'An opulent babu with a watch on chain was driving the carriage', an old Muslim was walking with a basket on head and not hearing the babu's loud shouts came in the way of the carriage; his basket's contents were all thrown into the road, he is saved but the chain-clad babu lashes his cane across the old man's face and uttering 'damned pig' drives away. He doesn't stop even at Gora's angry outcries. The old man begins to pick up his things that are left unspoilt; Gora joins him. He knows he is not showing kindness, yet passers-by would not understand that 'a *bhadralok* is trying to bring parity to the violated order of things by being beside a humiliated man to whom a wrongful insult has been doled out by another *bhadralok.*' Gora tries to disabuse the old Muslim's belief that the Allah would punish the guilty, by saying, 'one who puts up with wrong is also guilty, for he helps produce wrongdoings in the world.' Thus bit by bit the actual shape of India's reality is made part of Gora's experience. This is only the beginning.

But Gora has no dearth of argumentation. The ancient beliefs have kept such hold over his mind that he has no reason to call out to Bharatbarsha's women to arise and be awake, no matter how strongly in view of his new experience may Binoy argue with him. As caste differentiation is, so is man-woman differentiation an Indian truth to him. As the Brahmin (and of course he is thinking of the male) in his ideal Indian society is like a human god, so is woman '*pujārhā gṛhadīptayaḥ*' (venerable domestic light). What is interesting is that in order not to lose Gora's friendship Binoy goes on justifying his position to Pareshbabu and Sucharita. Not that he himself believes in all he says on Gora's behalf, but he tries so that Gora be not misunderstood. Pareshbabu once raises an issue that is particularly meaningful in the context of tradition versus modernity: 'I can't claim that I understand Bharatbarsha and I don't know for certain what Bharatbarsha wanted and if she got it, but can we ever go back to the days that are past?' Gora's answer to it in Binoy's words is: 'No truth can ever be past. Hence Bharatbarsha's truth has begun to move us. If one day even one of us can recognise and accept it as truth then the door to our energy trove will open—past's treasure will become present's possession.' But how about Gora's conservatism? Is it not a forced occupation of truth? Binoy too knows that 'Gora has a strong tendency to impose himself on others—he doesn't have the plain and simple peace that the bearers of truth should have.' But will Binoy openly own it? Perhaps Lalita has understood him right: 'He always tries to suppress his own doubt and opposition, lest he defies Gourmohanbabu. If one loves one can go along even against one's opinion—one can let oneself go without being blind—but that is not his case—maybe he follows Gourmohanbabu from love, but he cannot admit that at all.' In fact, to Sucharita now Gourmohan-less Binoy is no longer much important as he is to Lalita. How the two germs of love are germinating is seen through such assumed equations Binoy has with Gora.

But how about Gora himself? Does he not have a heart? True he loves Binoy, but the nature of that love is different. That is indeed an intense form of friendship—that friendship between two young men which is natural for youths without access to unrelated young women. The seed of the new love that is going to be sown in him soon is the love of man and woman by which he has seen Binoy to have been gripped, but of which he has himself been unconscious. But what is this happening to him now? 'Gora feels the presence of a lively being in the sky around him—on all sides his heart is being struck by the rolling waves of a heart, and he is bound by a certain intensity. Such wonderful feeling has never occurred to him before.' And we see the impact it has in the following Chapter (21): Gora does not go home straight as has been his habit but takes a long detour by the bank of Ganga. Nature which has never pulled him now overpowers him. Every single sentence of the first few paragraphs of this Chapter is significant. 'Alone in that darkness this intense feeling utterly disarms all his questions, all his hesitations. He begins to relish this new feeling of his with all his body and mind ….'

If this relish can be called his *sandhyasamgit* (evening song), then what happens to him the following morning is his *prabhatsamgit* (morning song). Leaving aside his personal feelings, he sets out to the dusty roads of India: a haversack on back, a stick in hand, and a few disciples for companions. The Bharatbarsha his heart cherishes, the Bharatbarsha that every once in a while shocks him with her battered images—it is to this Bharatbarsha that he journeys (like Vivekananda?). This is the first time that Binoy is not with him; this is the first time that he is really alone (the companions are superfluous and temporary). In other words, it is not a programme undertaken by their 'Hindu Welfare Society'; it is truly Gora's own search for India. This separation of Gora and Binoy is no longer a mere minor commotion resulting from their difference of character; it is probably going to be permanent. At the end of chapter 21 Anandamoyee 'calls upon God and prays—let Gora not have any unhappiness and let there be no cause for his real fissure from Binoy.' If we assume the novel *Gora* to be mainly the tale of Gora and Binoy, then we will have to pause here. Their paths now diverge.

These last days Gora has had a number of arguments with Haran. One main argument has been around the advance of the English people and, naturally, around the backwardness of Indians. In Haran's view, the English rule in India has been a stroke of fortune, 'God's dispensation'. Indians can only progress by imitating the English. The English-educated Indian who holds such a view is of course liked by the English. Haran does enjoy Magistrate Brownlowe's favour. This aspect of the ruler-ruled relationship is not to be overlooked in 19th century modernity, especially if the ruler is desirous like Brownlowe of having a good relation with the Indian gentry—accepting the invitation to their festivities for instance. But a true relationship rarely grows up—much of this is showing off—the ruler's pride as such is hardly ever diminished. He is eager to prove that the English want India's good. Since Brownlowe's wife is a missionary's daughter, Brownlowe believes that in order to enhance that good Indians should embrace Christianity. And he doesn't forget telling that to Haran. That Brownlowe's wife, during the farmers' fair to be held on the occasion of her husband's birthday, has invited Pareshbabu's daughters to recite and act out scenes from English poetry, especially in the presence of the Lieutenant Governor, does not in any way change the ruler-ruled relationship. For Brownlowe stays Brownlowe, a bad ruler. When Gora suddenly appears before him during his evening walk to tell him of the police oppression at Char-Ghoshpur village, he forgets all about matters related to Christ and God and threatens Gora: 'If in any way you interfere in Ghoshpur's affairs, you won't have an easy way out.' (The bad ruler's language does not really vary.) As Gora leaves after spiritedly declaring his intention—'I shall encourage the villagers to resist the police on their own'—he tells his companion in the evening walk, Haran, 'What signs are these among your compatriots?' Haran repeats his parrot's words about the incompleteness of English education and hence of the lack of the true religious spirit. No wonder he is an accomplice.

What Gora has seen in Char-Ghoshpur is anticipated in the first leg of his Bharat-journey: 'How alienated, how narrow, how weak this remote and huge Bharatbarsha is—how utterly unconscious she is of her powers and how fully ignorant of and how indifferent to her own good— … how big she takes things insignificant and how immovably hard to her is the least habit … by no means would Gora have imagined this if he had not stayed with the villagers.' But what has amazed Gora is the lack of reaction to all this in his travel companions—what is there to be surprised at, 'this is how the lower-class people are'. Motilal and Ramapati are direct proof of how the urban middle class is insensitive to rural Bharatbarsha. And the city is full of such Motilals and Ramapatis. Salvage of India is nothing but a slogan to them.

Char-Ghoshpur is the second leg of Gora's Bharat-journey. Gora sees in this Muslim village what he has not seen elsewhere, resistance to the oppression by white indigo planters. As a result all adult males are in either jail custody or absconding. The women are in a terrible shape being regularly harassed by the police. The only Hindu in the village is a barber who has given shelter to a Muslim boy in his house (a matter of great repulsion to Ramapati). The only brahmin of the region—in whose house can Gora and Ramapati bathe and eat—is the landlord's collector whose cruelty is endless and who has the police under control. Of course Gora cannot even think of that hospitality. Saying goodbye to Ramapati he goes back to that barber ('for a moment Ramapati looks and sees that Gora's tall body casting a short shadow in the terrible midday sun is alone walking back through the lonely hot sands'). But when he tells the barber that he would like to stay in his house for a few days so that he can give protection to the village, the barber's reply ('please forgive me, but if you try to protect us there will be no respite to us') repels him. For he is of the belief that if one fights for right wrong will be defeated. The barber's refusal to fight is proof of his cowardice. Gora has to wait long to comprehend Bharatbarsha's true reality. Scolding the collector and his buddy, the police inspector he goes to the headquarters, but before he reaches the news of his prying around reaches there. Brownlowe buckles himself up. He won't tolerate a native's battle 'for right'.

Forty-seven Char-Ghoshpur villagers are without trial behind bars. When Gora tries for their bail, Magistrate Brownlowe turns down the prayer, accomplishing his revenge on the native's defiance in the first round. The second round is provided by Gora himself through his headstrong nature by beating up the guard of the municipal tank for assaulting the students and going to police custody with them: Brownlowe sentences him to one month's rigorous imprisonment. Apropos Brownlowe's 'judgement' we may be reminded of 'a deputy of yore'—Gora had been told of him—who, on being asked by an English magistrate about his relatively liberal punishment of Indians, said, 'My dear sir, … the ones you send to prison are only cats and dogs to you, but the ones I send to prison are my brothers.' Was Tagore thinking of Bankim the Deputy?

And probably there were English magistrates once to listen to this. Even the Englishman on the steamer to Tribeni, who had initially been laughing with his English-educated Indian co-passenger at the harassment of the common pilgrims—Gora had gone up to scold them—while getting off came up to him and apologised. On the other hand, Mahim's new English boss at office is not only in looks but in manners too 'like a bulldog', though Mahim wouldn't hesitate to invite that boss to Sashimukhi's eventually materialised wedding. As an Englishman probably Brownlowe is somewhere in between the two kinds. The cause of his fury against Char-Ghoshpur's Muslim tenants must have been Pharu Sardar's breaking the indigo landlord's hand with his stick; but his reason for an extra degree of anger against Gora must have been Gora's courage and forthrightness when he came to talk to him on behalf of Char-Ghoshpur, in other words, his lack of a sense of inferiority—the kind that he found in Haran, for instance. In fact, Barodasundari's fuss about the invitation from Mrs. Brownlowe, to come and present her daughters' talent at her husband's birthday celebrations, smacks of the same sense of inferiority.

An epic-like novel keeps having new dimensions. With Brownlowe sentencing Gora it is no longer possible for Binoy to enjoy his hospitality as part of the team to perform at his birthday dinner; he takes the steamer to Kolkata. And when angry Lalita joins him as the steamer is about to start, things take a serious turn: though a Brahmo girl, emancipated to a degree, this amounts to her spending a night with an unrelated Hindu youth in the same steamer. Will 'society' take it easily, especially a 'society' that has Haran Chandra Nag for its 'headmaster'. Whatever Binoy and Lalita's own feelings are, it will get more and more complicated if not resolved at the level of 'society'. The Brahmos will go on whispering, writing letters to one another, and flashing it in their newspapers. More thrashings will have to be taken; and by Pareshbabu too, for he has been at the root of it. He is incapable of governing anyone in his family–that is, though a guardian he does not have Haran's guardian-like attitude–besides, it was he who had introduced Binoy and Gora to his home. In fact, it may jeopardise Haran's interests too, in case Sucharita's heart drifts away from him. Hence he insists on an early engagement ceremony between him and Sucharita. In the meantime another dimension has been added to the novel. When Barodasundari was away with her daughters at Brownlowe's birthday fair, Pareshbabu has given shelter to Sucharita's destitute aunt in the terrace room. The novel has told us at the outset that Sucharita and Satish are not Paresh's own offspring; he has raised them as his own after the untimely death of their parents. To him Sucharita is still the old Radharani (it was Baroda who had changed the old-fashioned 'Radharani' to 'Sucharita'). As Anandamoyee is Gora's mother without having given birth to him, so is Paresh Sucharita's father without being her actual parent. That motherhood and fatherhood are not merely biological, but are relationships of profound love and affection is never doubted or questioned in the novel.

That Gora's prison term is the third leg of his Bharat-journey is evident from the letter he writes to his mother from the police custody itself. 'Mother, I have learnt a lot this time by being exposed to the world. God knows, most of those who sit on judgement in this world are to be themselves pitied.

It is from the wrongdoings of those who do not get but give punishment that the prison-goers suffer. Many have together piled up the sin which the prisoners are expiating.' When Gora will come out of prison after a month, his disciples Abinash et al. will have no understanding at all of this experience of him: they will only shout victory to him and offer him garlands and thereby try to glorify themselves. And there is no dearth of Abinashes in Bharatbarsha. But Binoy is rare: 'Through the inconceivable rigours of prison his friend seems to have grown much bigger than a friend.' This one month Binoy too has not suffered little from a sadist institution called 'society' while protecting Lalita's honour—will Gora now recognise him? ('He does not seem to know how he is going to reveal today to Gora the one experience that has surpassed all others in this one month.') Will the paths of these two ever again meet—of these two 'sons' of Anandamoyee? In Gora's view Binoy marrying Lalita is defying *his* society, breaching the trust Bharatbarsha has put on him. Yet Binoy's not marrying Lalita is breaching another trust.

As to how fearful communal narrowness can be is proved not only by the arch Brahmo Haran—before firing the cannon ball against Lalita-Binoy's marriage he utterly defuses Lalita's enthusiastic effort to start a free girls' primary in the neighbourhood—but also by the Hindu widow Harimohini so confined to her rituals and so entrenched in her notions of pure and impure touch. Once she has her niece Sucharita in possession, her tooth and nail begin to show. After being settled in Sucharita's own house acquired through Pareshbabu's able management (of the money left him by Sucharita's father), she has forgotten how she came seeking shelter and as a prelude to that prayer, what she had written to Sucharita. That is indeed a story by itself, of a widowed woman, humiliated and oppressed by her in-laws, swindled by her own son-in-law and the indirect cause of her daughter's death, treacherously deprived of her portion in the family property by her husband's younger brothers, eventually a destitute living off charity in a holy place. Yet she is now eager to find a groom for Sucharita from her in-laws' family and is thus scheming that Sucharita's property be annexed to her in-laws'. Her grabbing attitude to keep a hold over Sucharita is no longer out of affection but of greed in the interest of her in-laws' family—a family that she now upholds on reasons of power and pedigree. Harimohini is a striking example of how a superstitious Hindu woman can be subservient, in spite of all oppression and treachery, to the male-dominated Hindu society. The most distorted reality of the ideal of Indian society that Gora carries in his heart is indeed seen in Harimohini who was once so docile, almost tumbled in dust, but now so immodest and conscious of her rights. Losing everything she had at one time taken refuge at the feet of her idol Gopiballabha; now comforted by her possessions her Gopiballabha has turned into a mere habit. It does not matter if her offerings to Gopiballabha fall short, as long as she can aspire to take full possession of Sucharita along with her property. And what can be more anachronistic and absurd than the instrument she uses for that purpose (meaning her youngest brother-in-law whom she invites over, a widower and utterly property-minded and the antipodes of Sucharita in every way)? Harimohini is the living instance of the fact that not everyone burning in the flames of sorrow is purified. She did get a God-sent opportunity of becoming

Sucharita's mother from Sucharita's aunt; she misses it and loses it to Anandamoyee. She is indeed a village incarnation of the Brahmo Baroda; she is a hundred and eighty degrees away from the Hindu Anandamoyee.

Back from prison, when he has been going out regularly to nearby villages Gora has seen many superstitious people like Harimohini entirely controlled by age-old customs. 'It is doubtful if such fear-prone, helpless creatures, unable to determine their own good are seen elsewhere in the world. … What is *not* to be done has, through prohibitions in every step, bound their nature in a regular mesh. … Gora cannot help seeing that by using the weapon of custom one man is draining another man's blood and cruelly rendering him a pauper. … This (Hindu) society does not help man in his need, does not stand by him in his distress, only bending him by prohibitions endangers him. Gora comes to notice so clearly the ill outcome of such foolish compulsions that it becomes impossible for him to delude himself in the magic web of sentimentality.' Among Muslims on the other hand Gora sees a unity which comes from religion, not from rituals alone. 'As on the one side their actions are not all ritual-bound, so on the other side their religious tie is most intimate.' Going round from village to village Gora sees the truth in its bare form, but that does not dissuade him from his ideals.

Quite early in the novel Anandamoyee had once tried to convince Krishnadayal about why it was necessary to let Gora know his true identity. Krishnadayal refused to be convinced, for he was afraid of its reaction at the levels of society and government. Towards the end of the novel, in Chapter 63, when Gora is trying to dissuade Anandamoyee from participating in

Binoy's wedding ('Mother, you will have to remember that you belong to society and do have a debt to it.'), Anandamoyee again raises the issue with Krishnadayal ('It is not right even a single more day to let Gora continue in his delusion, this is going too far.'). Krishnadayal has the same answer as before ('If it is revealed now I will be liable to answering a lot.')—his wish is to keep it hidden till his death, what happens afterwards does not bother him. Very selfish and irresponsible indeed as if all responsibility in the long run is Anandamoyee's who took up the newly-born motherless Gora to her lap. Anandamoyee incidentally raises the matter of Krishnadayal's health—with his hard ever esoteric practices is he not turning into thin air? There may be a hint in this that his death may not be too far. In other words, the fact of Gora being called to Krishnadayal's bedside before performing his much publicised 'expiatory rites' may not be all that sudden. That is, the novel is not delivering a punch to the turn of events. Besides, when Gora being enmeshed in his own flow of words is on his way to embrace *sannyas*—without listening to the murmurs against it from his inner self or heart—is the right moment for him to learn the circumstances of his birth or his actual 'identity'.

On learning the circumstances of his birth 'all his life in a single moment seems to be a very strange dream to Gora. … He does not seem to feel who he is, where he is. There does not seem to have been a thing called past behind him, and the future he has so long projected for himself with a single-minded determination is totally wiped out. He seems to be floating like a moment's dew on a lotus leaf. He has no mother, no father, no country, no race, no name, no ancestral initiator, he has no deity. He has only a universal "No".' All his 'Yes' for so many years has blown away at a moment's breath, he is no longer an 'I'. Not being 'I' means he has no longer a 'You' or a 'He' or 'She' to deal with. All that remains is his existence, the feeling that he *is* and in the midst of his widespread 'Nothingness' that seems to be a wakening. As if he has been asleep all this while and while asleep, dreaming, now he has woken up. Woken up where? On Bharatbarsha's soil ('This dawn with a totally bared heart I have been born in Bharatbarsha's lap.'). Going over to Pareshbabu he tells him of this dream and this awakening: 'In order to build an unblemished unswerving idealised Bharatbarsha and inside that impenetrable fortress, to protect my devotion fully safely, what struggles have I not put forth all this while with all around! Today at a moment's blast that fortress of mine of ideals has tumbled down like a dream. Being utterly freed I have all of a sudden arrived at a great truth. All Bharatbarsha's wellbeing and ill, happiness and sorrow, knowledge and ignorance have come absolutely to my heart's doors—today I have won the rights of true service—the true field of work has unfurled in front of me …' It is his existence born out of 'Nothingness' that has brought Gora to this field of work. 'What I was trying day and night to become, yet could not, I have today become. I am today an Indian. Inside me there is no strife with any society, Hindu or Muslim or Christian.' The reader may not fall in with this somewhat existentialist reading putting together excerpts from Chapters 76 and 77, but will surely not doubt Gora's awakening.

One wants to go over the last pages of this novel again and again. And at the very end tears rise in the eyes: what immense emotion yet how controlled! There are five paragraphs in the Appendix, but the sentences are only ten. Words are first spoken by Gora: 'Mother, *you* are my mother. The very mother I had been seeking around was waiting for me in my home. You have no caste, you don't accuse, you don't hate anyone—you are the very image of good. *You* are my Bharatbarsha.' The last words are Anandamoyee's: 'in a tearful voice gently she speaks into Gora's ears: "Gora, let me send for Binoy now."' The gulf that he had laid with Binoy out of mis-judgement is of course no longer there. The novel had begun with Binoy, now by taking Binoy's name the novel is ending. There is no need to stretch the narrative any further. Perhaps like the Dostoyevsky of *Crime and Punishment* Tagore does not even have to say that Gora's tale now moves in a different trail.

'I am a Hindu. Hindus are not a community. Hindus are a people. This people are so large that the essence of their peoplehood cannot be limited by a single definition. As the ocean is not waves, so are Hindus not a community.' It is needless to say that these are Gora's words. He was still unaware of the circumstances of his birth; his 'identity' has not been attained. 'I am a Hindu' is how he knows himself, and how he lets others know him. After attaining his 'identity' the second thing he will tell Pareshbabu is 'I am *not* a Hindu'. And the last thing he will tell him is: 'Please initiate me with the *mantra* of that very God Who is of Hindus, Muslims,

Christians, Brahmos, everyone's—Whose temple doors are never shut to any people, any person, never ever—Who is not Hindus' God alone, Who is Bharatbarsha's God.' True before he attained his 'identity' there was nothing lacking in his perception of Bharatbarsha, but his Bharatbarsha was a Hindu Bharatbarsha. We remember how he had been initiated into this Bharatbarsha as outcome of a debate with a Christian missionary. And he argued forever with Brahmos because they had dishonoured that Hindu Bharatbarsha, had deserted her. He was even about to give up his boyhood friend because he was marrying a Brahmo girl. The idea of the '*Mahamanab'* or 'Great Man' as embodied in *Gitanjali* 106 (written in 1910) would be beyond his imagination. Yet there was no alloy in his Hindutva, in his allegiance to Hindu Bharatbarsha.

Gora before the revelation of his 'identity' sometimes reminds us of Brahmabandhab Upadhyay. He too was marked by his allegiance to Hindu Bharatbarsha and by good deeds for that purpose. His aim was India's freedom (when in early youth his two trips to the Gwalior kingdom to take martial training failed, Bhabanicharan Bandyopadhyay took up the pen for weapon). Keeping his Hindutva intact he was attracted to the Brahmo Samaj, became Keshab Sen's devotee and at one point took conversion to the latter's 'Nababidhan' or New Dispensation. His later conversion to Christianity, first Protestantism, then Catholicism (his change of name from Bhabanicharan Bandyopadhyay to Brahmabandhu > Brahmabandhab Upadhyay was done at that time) was also without dislodging his Hindu roots. He soon came to be known not only as a Hindu-Catholic but a Catholic-Vedantin occasioning, after Vivekananda's death, a preacher's voyage to England. However, on return his main mission turned out to be extremist nationalism carried out through his evening daily *Sandhya*. When for printing seditious staff he was put in the dock, he admitted to the printing through his advocate Chittaranjan Das, but refused to be tried by alien law for his God-appointed task of attaining his country's *Swaraj*. Born the same year as Tagore, it was he who first called Tagore a 'world-poet'. He wrote a review of Tagore's book of poems *Naivedya*—the first ever serious and appreciative reading of Tagore's poetry—became his associate in founding the Bhrahmacharyashram at Santiniketan, and was also the first to call him 'Gurudev'. Much later in the introduction written by Tagore named 'Abhas' (Cue) to *Char Adhyay* the emphasis was on Brahmabandhab's last words to him during a sudden visit to him probably in 1907, the year of his untimely death: 'Rabibabu, I have utterly fallen.' From one point of view *Char Adhyay* is the story of such a fall. Brahmabandhab then was memory. But the moment when Tagore began his *Gora* Brahmabandhab was every bit alive and famous. Should not the respect and wonder expressed at the outset of 'Abhas' ('I was profoundly attracted to his extraordinary dedication and intellect in spiritual matter; … I am still full of wonder remembering how, while often taking a stroll on the village path near the *ashram* and discussing with me, he would explicate the most difficult theories.') have an impact on his *writing*? For instance, does not the expiation done by Brahmabandhab for his personal purification have some resemblance with Gora's projected expiation piercing which his 'identity' materialises?

It may be that in writing up *Gora* Tagore filtered his perceptions of Brahmabandhab with those of Sister Nivedita.

We have been ever told that Nivedita was Gora's probable source of inspiration. But which Gora, the one who did not know that he was Irish by birth, or the one who came to know that he was Irish by birth, yet who dedicated himself to the service of Bharatbarsha he had cherished since birth? Probably Tagore found his inspiration for this second Gora in Nivedita. Patriotism was not a biological factor to him. I am born of Indian parents and so I will love India, is not necessarily true; it may give birth to nationalism, but not love of my country. That is born in the conscious mind. Probably Tagore took Nivedita as a symbol of that conscious mind. This becomes evident in the essay he wrote after Nivedita's death named 'Sister Niveditā' (1911)—later included in his book of essays called *Parichay*. 'In no one else have I seen this wondrous power to so utterly dedicate oneself.' It is wrong to think that Nivedita was able to make this dedication because she was a 'Hindu at heart'; that may add to *our* glory but does not help understand Nivedita. This is a little like what Krishnadayal told Gora to dissuade him from his resolve to perform expiatory rites: 'You think you have made your entry into Hinduism, but that is wholly your illusion. … Every drop of your blood, from your head to foot is opposed to it.' 'In fact, if we try to find out how much Hindu she (Nivedita) was we are bound to have many impediments—in other words, I do not think it true that she was at the same stage of Hinduhood as we are. If the historical and scientific way she looked at Hinduism cum Hindu society—by penetrating the immovable wall of scriptural immanence, and with a mind free from superstitions thoughtfully and imaginatively followed its course through many changes and expressions—be adopted by us, then the very foundation of what everybody calls Hinduhood today will crumble.... We should revere her not because she was a Hindu, but because she was a great person.... Other Europeans too have been seen to have embraced Bharatbarsha's burden as their life's burden, but ... they have not been able to offer themselves respectfully.... But Sister Nivedita with ardent love and utter respect offered herself to Bharatbarsha, she did not keep the least bit of herself in hand.'

It is needless to say that as much as Brahmabandhab so is Nivedita only an inspiration, not a rationale for Gora's career. Besides, the novel *Gora* is not merely Gora's tale, there are others in it—some not even connected to Gora, for instance, Harimohini and her brother-in-law Kailas. There are also events which Gora does not motivate, for instance, Binoy and Lalita's love and marriage. Also, though Mahim is Gora's elder brother, his lifestyle is independent of Gora. And on the prospects behind his daughter Sashimukhi's marriage proposal not a very short shadow is cast by 'society'. Gora is a Hindu; Mahim is also a Hindu, but how different! Again, Gora is a Hindu, his disciple Abinash too is a Hindu, yet how different they are—Abinash will agree being a groom, but the dowry as per society's 'dictates' will be collected by his father. On the other hand, in the Hindu-Brahmo debate, Haran is no less fanatical than Gora; whether Gora be there or not, Haran will be—his 'self-confidence' from religious reasons will permit him any amount of bad deeds. Who else in this novel is as adamant as he is? Does Tagore at one point towards the end abandon him, as Dostoyevsky did, though in the middle, his Luzhin in *Crime and Punishment*? In addition, this novel is a tale of the Kolkata of 1880s—it begins with a note on that and surely we cannot overlook the two opening sentences of Chapter 2: 'In this evening of the rainy season the sky's darkness being drenched seems to have gone heavy. Under the silent aegis of colourless and monotonous clouds the Kolkata city, like a huge unhappy dog mutely burrowing its nozzle in the tail, is curled up (a very urban simile).' Or those two familiar sentences from the opening of chapter 21: 'Kolkata's Ganga and Ganga's banks being invaded in water and land by the ugliness of mercantile civilisation's profiteering greed had not yet put on the shackles of railways on the shore and a bridge over the river. In the winter evening then the city's polluted breath had not covered the sky with such intensity.' If we so wish, we may also draw up a mental map of the Kolkata of the novel—that may not be all that less than Balzac's Paris or Dostoyevsky's St. Petersburg. That a novel is not just a course of events and its subject-object-agency, but also its place, is proved by *Gora* too as by many other modern 'epics'.

2014

The 'Individual' and the 'Universe' in Tagore

The 'Individual' and the 'Universe' are categories that a philosopher alone can handle. Being the least philosophically equipped I can only take a look at Tagore's non-reflective writings in search of tropes related to such experience. My search will have an initial handicap of being at one remove since I shall be speaking of Tagore's classics in a language to which his originals do not easily lend. Falling back upon such writings as *Sadhana* or *The Religion of Man* would of course have helped me, but to speak of him solely on the basis of what can be called his supplementary *oeuvre* addressed to an audience that doesn't understand Bengali, would indeed be unusual for one who happens to speak his language. On that count I may be accused of essentialism, but I would rather accept it than overlook his primary *oeuvre*.

Let me begin by quoting a song dated 1885 (*e moha aabaran khule daao*), a *brahmasamgit* that in spite of its tone of worship touches on our theme. Here is my loose rendering:

> Lord, this veil of illusion
> tear off.

Let me see your beautiful face
with all eyes,
look into my heart, O Lord,
look.

I wish I could add its score to show how compelling its tune was. (*Song No. 170 in Tagore's Collected Works, Vol. 4, West Bengal Government, 1987*)

Even if we hear an echo of Īśopaniṣad in it, it introduces the noun 'veil' or 'veil of illusion' and the verb 'tear off' that are going to recur a hundred times in him, again and again, and throughout his life. The 'veil' or the 'veil of illusion' is his who is speaking, the first person or the poet's persona. The 'tearing off' is to be done by the one who is addressed, the second person, the 'Lord' whose face, 'beautiful face', will then be seen. 'Look inside my heart' is perhaps the more immediate item of worship, but the moot point has been already made, the tearing off by 'you' of 'my' veil of illusion.

This may take us at random to Song 773 (*e je more aabaran*) dated 1913 whose first movement, loosely again, is:

My veil *is* this.
But it tears off in no time.
At one breath it flies away
if *you* so will.

This is not a prayer. The 'you' here is more familiar, not the 'Lord' of the earlier song. The 'breath' is of course the breath of 'you', potent enough but subject to motivation. The familiarity of the first person's tone in addressing the second person maintains in the other movements, though a change occurs towards the end in the former hailing the latter as 'Lord'. In fact that cognition turns out to be the logical outcome of the tearing off or rather, the flying away of the veil. That logic is more explicit in the following song from a year later (*e aabaran kshay habey go kshay habe*…):

> This veil shall tear off, oh, tear off, and
> this body and mind have the ultimate bliss.
> Illusion's shadow shall shatter off the eyes,
> the cosmic lotus shall bloom in my heart,
> it is you, my Lord, this life shall hail.
> My veins shall dance to the cosmic beat,
> my heart shall gain an immense life.
> It shall vibrate with your light-lute's strings,
> and be pendant from your star-gems' chain,
> its desires all squandering and annihilating.

(Song 978)

We have details here of a closer consequence. The original of 'ultimate bliss' is '*bhumananda*' that has a sure metaphysical connotation. One of the Sanskrit phrases Tagore never tires of quoting is '*bhūmaiva sukham*' preceded by '*nālpe sukhamasti*'. This is not to put forward the case of him as a metaphysician drawing on the Upanishads, but to make home his longing for a larger reality. The 'illusion' is of course '*maya*', another metaphysical item, but its shadow to shatter off the eyes is a physical enough experience. My 'cosmic' is an apology for '*visva*' which is used twice, conjunct respectively with 'lotus' (= '*kamal*') and 'beat' (= '*tal*'). The latter would take us ahead to a later song (No. 1486 dated 1926/27), the famous 'Beats of dance, O Nataraj' ('*nrityer taale taale he Nataraaj*') equally famed for its accompanying choreography. The former too may take us back to an earlier song (No. 836 dated 1912) though of a slightly different thrust: 'I had no knowledge the day the lotus bloomed, / my mind was elsewhere' ('*je din phutlo kamal kichhui jaani naai*'). This is not merely to register Tagore's self-intertextuality, but also to recognise his unity of poetic vision. The two metaphors, 'light-lute' ('*aalo-binaa*') and 'star-gems' (*taaraamani*'), that come at the end of the song, are obviously in tune with the spirit of the '*visvakamal*' and '*visvataal*'.

'Have you made up with your own self this veil for yourself' ('*aapnaare diye rachili re ki e aapnaari aabaran*') (Song 1425 dated 1926) is a statement of central importance to our theme of the 'individual' and the 'universe'. 'Self' being a veil to 'self', gives two meanings to the self, the smaller self or ego and the larger self or being, '*aham*' and '*aatmaan*', as Tagore elaborates in his essay on 'Manusher Dharma' or 'The Human Essence'. The last poem of one of his last books, written in the year of his death, begins with the following words: *e aamir aabaran sahaje skhalita hoye jaak*:

> Let this self shed its scales at ease,
> soul's white light
> pierce all mists and
> unveil the truth's undying form.

(Arogya 33)

A conflict is quoted next between men in the plural and an eternal man in the singular whom he has earlier called the '*visvamaanab*' (the universal man) or '*amitamaanab*' (the man beyond measure) or '*paramamaanab*' (the ultimate man). By no means is the latter an aggregate of the former: it lies within and needs be invoked. This conflict is thus between 'this I' ('*ei aami*') and 'that I' ('*sei aami*'), the outer 'I' and the inner 'I'.

If we think of the span rather casually hinted here between 1885 and 1941, we realise the urgency he had felt from time to time of reaching down or out to the truth that is of universal significance. And he knew that he couldn't do it without the veil of the self being lifted or its scales shed. A song in which this is most succinctly expressed, without recourse to any metaphysics as in its immediate successor, Song 978 quoted above, in other words, in purely poetic terms, is Song 977 ('*aapan hote baahir hoye baaire daanraa*') dated 1914 quoted above in part:

> Come from within self and stand out,
> in your heartbeat you will hear the universe.
> Let this mighty surge of waves
> break into a dance in you, and
> let all your senses shake.
> O you, bee, sit here on this blue
> being gold-splattered in sun-dust.
> Unfurl your wings
> in the boundless sky,
> you will have a free play with All.

Perhaps this 'All' will be further understood if we contrast it with Faust's hunger for 'everything', small and big, in Goethe, Tagore's peer in versatility. Faust's hunger leads him to the famous pact with Mephistopheles who threatens him with sloth cum happiness. Being an allegory of 'striving' and concomitant 'erring' it deals with irreconcilable antinomies, whereas what Tagore is looking for is the universe manifest in the individual. There is room for epiphany in him, as he himself describes one on seeing the sunrise from Sudder Street's balcony, or that pervasive joy, recalled later in 1933, on one morning during his days by River Padma in the late 1880s and early 1890s: 'On my way to bath I stopped a moment at the window out of sheer curiosity. Instantly that one moment became vast. My eyes filled up with tears. I felt like falling down to someone's feet in utter submission. Who is this so dear to me who gathers my passing moments into his everlasting time?'—*Manusher Dharma*: 'Manabsatya [The Human Truth] 3'. It might have been the same or a similar experience that he had invoked in his 'autobiographical' *Talk in China*: 'The feeling which I had was like what a man, groping through a fog without his destination, might feel when he suddenly discovers that he stands before his house.'[1] Yes, epiphany or momentary revelation, but never placidity, never a claim to permanence turning him into a modern-day Mira as it were singing and dancing on to her Giridhari Nagar. In Goethe's Faust's case it ends in epiphany cum happiness, but being happiness in anticipation of happiness, no sloth (and hence, in spite of the contraband words – '*Verweile doch, du bist so schön*' – the coveted damnation has to misfire for Mephisto and we have to

1 *The English Writings of Rabindranath Tagore*, Vol. 2, *ed. cit*., p. 590.

have a retake of 'Das Ewig-Weibliche' reverting at the same time to the redoubtable 'Prolog im Himmel'.

If by humanism is meant man at the centre and the rest on the periphery, then Goethe's *Faust* is a humanist document. During their pact making, when Mephisto reminds Faust that though he, Mephisto, will be Faust's servant on earth, beyond earth Faust will be Mephisto's servant, Faust readily retorts that he has no interest in the beyond, that his joys only derive from this earth ('*Aus dieser Erde quillen meine Freuden*' l. 1683). Faust by definition is an atheist. Tagore's humanism, if we can call it humanism at all, is quite different. His man is the universal man, endowed with individual humanity in every respect, *man* in thought, action and speech, yet fully prone to transcendence, not necessarily God-crazy, but given unto something larger and pervasive. He is as much in love with nature as with fellow human beings, sees more harmony than discord around, and doesn't count on a telos to crown it all. Happiness is not what comes at the end but is revealed on the way through a sense of rhythm where sorrow too has its part. Seasons are a fitting symbol of that rhythm, and it is not a coincidence that the postmen in *Dakghar* (*The Post Office*) in whom Amal is especially interested for the letter they may bring him from the King, have such names as Badal (rains) and Sarat (early autumn).

Naturally with such symbolism built in, the language has to have a second register. Rabindranath's image of the King, for instance, from *Saradotsab* (*Autumn-Festival*) to *Raja* (*The King of the Dark Chamber*) to *Dakghar* cannot possibly be viewed without reference to it. In fact Amal's foster father's or the Headman's confinement to realism in *Dakghar*, the former's with obvious pathos and the latter's with a touch of malicious glee, is its necessary contrast, though the play's last words ('Sudha hasn't forgotten you') carry an ambivalence beyond that realism. But this register seems to be at its most active in the riddles that some of the characters in his plays speak in, almost as their natural turn of speech. They tend to take logic by its throat to arrive at a perception of truth. Thakurda the grandfather in *Raja* is famous for that. When his companions give vent to their doubt about their King's existence by quoting their losses, he quotes his own loss which is bigger than everybody else's, but says that he wouldn't add to that loss by losing his King ('You still have two sons left—but I have lost all five of mine one by one, not a single son left!' 'So?' 'What do you mean? The sons are gone, and you want me to quarrel with my King and lose him too?'). It is he who reminds them of the song 'We are all *king* in our King's kingdom, / else, with what worth shall we meet him?' ('*aamraa sabaai raajaa aamaader ei raajaar raajatve*') The riddling continues in such words as 'We do whatever *we* wish, / yet it's his wish we move to', or 'We shall go *our* way, / but be at end on *his* way.' Such freedom and such faith are apparently contradictory, but only apparently, not in truth. Indeed the inner logic is not far from that of Īśopaniṣad's '*tadejati tannaijati taddūre tadvantike*' which, we are told, when quoted by Tagore, made an impact on the physicist Heisenberg of the 'Uncertainty Principle' at their meeting in Kolkata in 1928.

Apropos riddles, we have already spoken of the *baul* Dhananjay Bairagi, first appearing in the play *Prayaschitta* (Expiation) but more fully, in *Muktadhara* (*The Waterfall*), whose followers are ever baffled by his seeming unreason. He would lead and fight for their cause, ready to bear any amount of beating for that, but stop them from brute retaliation. Perhaps his most remarkable riddle for them, as quoted above, is when the news of Prince Abhijit's self-sacrifice to free the dammed up current to give them back their water, arrives at the end of the play and they bemoan that they had come in search of him and would now never find him, he tells them that now they had found him for ever. Nothing can be truer.

Can we then say that in such truths lies Tagore's perception of the individual's relation to the universe, or rather, of the universe as manifest in the individual? In other words, can this eventually take us to his concept of the universal man? Perhaps we can now understand why he couldn't agree with Einstein's notion of an ultimate universe independent of human perception. Nothing to him is independent of man, not even God. Say we call this 'Universal Humanism' implying a certain steadiness of vision; but does it sustain to the end of his life? Judging by his last poems, we may not say so, at least not readily. He never loses his faith in man, but does his universe withstand questionings regarding its affability? Among his very last poems is one, the starkest perhaps, that just records a 'No':

> First day's sun
> asked
> at Being's new appearance
> who are you,
> *no* answer came.
> Years went by,
> last sun of the day

last question utters on the western seashore,
at silent evening—
who are you,
gets *no* answer..

(27 July 1941: morning. Rendering based on Amiya Chakravarty's translation in A Tagore Reader, *ed. cit.: emphasis added)*

How far are we from Rigveda's *Nāsadīya Sūkta* that begins with '*nāsad āsīnno sad āsīt tadānīm'* (Then neither Being nor Non-Being was—10.129.1)?

2011 (in Sanchari, *Bengali Department Journal, Vivekananda College for Women, Kolkata, 2016)*

'If my heart's doors are ever shut'

Our celebration of the hundred years of the handing over of the Nobel Prize to Rabindranath Tagore on 29 January 1914 at the Government House, Kolkata, is a reminder that he was primarily a poet. It is a necessary reminder, for we have recently had his other aspects overshadow the poetry. Talking of *Gitanjali*: *Song Offerings* has been either routine or a mere recall of what had happened a century ago. There has been little rereading. Is it a classic in the sense of a museum piece, to praise and pass by, or a classic indeed that comes alive every time we approach it? Bengalis, both Indian and Bangladeshi as well as diasporic, still cherish some of their originals as songs, though doubt persists as to which precede, tunes or words. Non-Bengali Indians may also follow suit to an extent in some translation in their language, when available. But as such, the poetry is taken for granted. Of course I am speaking of the general reception, for there have been singular appreciations, whether from the purely poetic or from a more philosophical than poetic, angle, as an instance of the existentialist 'nothing' for example, or in terms of the interplay of an 'I' and a 'you'. Indeed this last is a regular cue to any reader who approaches the poems without any preconceptions.

As to the non-Bengali non-Indian reception to the *Song Offerings*, the translation is often held dated (though few surpass a line like 'Ages pass, and still thou pourest, and still there is room to fill' or 'Clouds heap upon clouds and it darkens'), which is only an argument for newer translations, in fact newer and newer, for no translation is ever definitive. A few hands have already been there, which again is no argument that there may not be more. My tentative and inept attempts from the *Gitanjali* cycle—in which I add *Naivedya* and *Kheya* to the three song-clusters, namely, *Gitanjali*, *Gitimalya* and *Gitali*—are in part coloured by the 'I'-'you' approach. Surely, a few of them are beside the *Song Offerings*' scope, but as such they continue the *Song Offerings'* spirit. Also I have avoided texts translated by Tagore himself, in either the *Song Offerings* or elsewhere. Mine are *Naivedya* 5 and 21; *Kheya*: only a few lines from 'Ghater Path' and 'Prabhate'; *Gitanjali* 12, 28, 59, 60 and 118; *Gitimalya* 86, 101 and 103; *Gitali* 4, 5, 16, 33, 38 and 70. I am going to quote only a few of them here to illustrate my reading. First, *Naivedya* 5 from which I have borrowed my essay's title:

> If my heart's doors
> are ever shut,
> smash them open and enter,
> do not go back, my lord.
>
> If ever in my *veena*
> your darling name is not struck,

do kindly stay a moment
and do not go back, my lord.

If ever at your call
my torpor is not broken,
wake me up with thunder,
do not go back, my lord.

If ever in your place
I put someone else,
you, my prince for ever
do not go back, my lord.

(jadi e aamaar hridayduaar
bandha rahe go kabhu)

'My lord' is a literal rendering of '*prabhu'*. It would be idle to speculate on the identity of this '*prabhu*' or on the other hand, to feel shy of him. Let us not forget that Tagore had already written *brahmasamgits* to be formally sung at Brahmo festivals. Let us not also forget that *Naivedya* (1901) was dedicated to his father, the Great Brahmo.

Surely, we would not call *Naivedya* 5 a straight prayer, there being a discourse in it. 'I' is talking to 'you', urgently no doubt, but in relatively familiar terms and expecting a response. 'You' is not the formal 'Lord' of *brahmasamgit*s, but a 'lord' that knows 'I' with his possible torpor. In other words, a relationship exists, no matter how unequal. Another poem with footfalls ringing in the heart, *Gitali* 4 is further from a prayer:

I have laid a road in my heart,
there falls foot,
there falls your foot.
And so my life's fibres
are all trembling with pain
trembling with tremor.
On pain's road you travel,
your foot kisses pain,
and my seeking is full of weeping
for ever
lifelong.

Seeing my tears flood
I no longer fear, I
no longer fear.
Death-pull by pulling me
will take me across,
and I shall cross the ocean.
Storm winds at a howl
are blowing your way,
my boat sinks, I'll jump overboard
and be at your feet,
hugging them I'll survive.

(aami hridayete path ketechhi
sethaay charan pare
tomaar sethaay charan pare.)

There is a recognition in this poem of the necessity of pain in the 'I'-'you' relationship. It is not merely 'I''s pain, but also in his own way 'you''s, which reminds us of *Song Offerings* 45: 'Every moment and every age, every day and every night he comes, comes, ever comes.' Or of *Song Offerings* 23: 'By what dim shore of the ink-black river, by what far edge of the frowning forest, through what mazy depth of gloom art thou threading thy course to come to me, my friend?' Besides, the storm is a regular motif in the *Gitanjali* cycle, often in conformity with the crossing in a boat, or even as such, as in *Gitali* 33:

On the way, my lonely way,
the lamp went out.
A storm is gathered, oh look,
the storm is now my companion.
In corners of sky, a dreadful laughter
is ringing every moment, and doom
is rummaging through my hair and clothes.

The way I was on
is lost.
I shall have to find another
in the dark.
Perhaps the thunder
will tell me,
and tell in which abode
will night break into dawn.

(jete jete eklaa pathe
nibhechhe mor baati,
jhar esechhe, ore, ebaar
jharke pelem saathi.)

Is not this enough to end the rumour that the 'tryst' in Tagore is effete? It was customary at one time to distinguish the poetry of the way from that of arrival. In this song and in a great many others, Tagore fits in with the former. 'I' strives towards 'you' or waits for 'you', both bearing a hint of anxiety. I know that I am using a loaded word, but this anxiety is more out of eagerness than despair. The theme of waiting may bring Kafka to our mind. But Kafka's and Tagore's are two different worlds. In one we end on futility, in the other on hope. The Man from the country ('Mann vom Lande') in the seminally located parable 'Before the Law' ('Vor dem Gesetz') in *Trial* (*Der Prozess*) waits all his life in front of an open door seeking entry, to be told at dying of the imminent shutting of the door that had been meant for him alone. On the other hand in Tagore we have:

> This moonlight night they have all gone to the woods
> carried away by spring's drunken breeze.
> I shall not go, oh, I shall not,
> I shall stay in my room,
> be here in my lone corner.
> I shall not go out in this drunken breeze.
>
> My room with great care
> I have to wash and clean.
> And I have to stay up,
> who knows when he will come
> if he once remembers me.
> I shall not go out in this drunken breeze.

> *(Gitimalya 86)*
> *(aaj jyotsnaaraate sabaai gechhe bane*
> *vasanter ei maataal samirane.)*

This song with a haunting tune has words that show determination, as opposed perhaps to the touching despondency of the Man from the country towards the very end of his waiting in the parable in *Trial* (begging the very lice on the Doorman's clothes to speak on his behalf to the Doorman to let him enter).

'I shall not go out in this drunken breeze': 'I' does not know when 'he' (replacing the familiar 'you' without much dent on the relationship) will or, for that matter, at all, come, for that depends on his remembering 'I'. But that does not deter 'I' from keeping ready.

We may recall the twin poems in *Kheya*, 'Subhakshan' and 'Tyag', translated by Tagore into one (*The Gardener* 7), where the young girl stresses her need to dress up for the Prince to pass her door that day. But she knows that 'he will not glance up once at my window', that 'he will pass out of my sight in the twinkling of an eye'. Her later admission that she could not but throw her ruby chain from the neck as the Prince was passing by, to be only crushed by his wheels ('no one knows what my gift was and to whom'), has no less a sense of conviction—conviction and not despair, perhaps even a touch of fulfilment. We are far from Kafka's world especially signified by the aphorism: 'Crows maintain that a single crow could destroy heavens. True, but that proves nothing against heavens, for heavens only mean the impossibility of crows.'

However, this does not rule out the possibility of indifference in the scheme of things as seen in the poem 'Anabashyak' (from *Kheya*) discussed above. But that dark mood too is balanced by such lines as:

> These are your cattle of lights then
> these suns and stars by scores;
> from where do you play your pipe
> to graze them in upper skies?
> Rows of grasses raising heads,
> green leaves in trees' branches,
> they are light-grazing cattle
> crowding in flowers and fruits.
>
> In mornings far afar
> they run raising dust.
> In dark at dusk
> you bring them back to fold.
> My hopes and desires
> are all profuse and abroad,
> O my life's shepherd
> will you call me in at dusk?
>
> (*Gitimalya* 103)
> (*ei to tomaar aalok-dhenu*
> *suryataaraa dale dale—*
> *kothaay bose baajaao benu,*
> *charaao mahaa gagantale*.)

What man needs is to be grazed along with everything else, from the tiniest grasses to the brightest suns, in other words, to be part of all. There is a line in a song in the play *Achalayatan* (1912: The Immovable Precincts), not the one included in *Song Offerings* (57): 'I have opened all doors today / to go and be full with all'. We hear an echo of that in the following lines: *aapan hote baahir hoye baaire daanraa./ buker maajhe visvaloker paabi saaraa.*:

> Come from within self
> and stand out,
> in your heartbeat you
> will hear the universe.
> Let this mighty surge of waves
> break into a dance in you, and
> all your senses shake—
> stand out, stand out. (from *Gitali* 70)

This reminds us of another poem, *Gitanjali* 59 where the poet is telling the Great Poet to take over from him, that is, the small poet's ever so loud repertoire, and make music with his life itself:

> Now put to silence
> your effusive poet.
> Snatch his heart-flute
> and play it yourself at depths.
> With dead-of-night's deepest tunes
> pour resonance into the flute,
> the resonance with which you astonish
> the moon and planets.

> Let all that is scattered of me
> over life and death,
> by your music's pull come
> and be together at your feet.
> Many days' words
> will instantly float away, and alone
> I shall hear your flute
> in boundless dark.
>
> (*ebaar nirab kore daao he tomaar*
> *mukhar kabire,*
> *taar hridaybaansi aapni kere*
> *baajaao gabhire.*)

Once again the identity of 'you' is not an immediate issue: it could very well be the cosmic order to which belong the moon and planets. We may even invoke Pythagoras' 'music of the spheres'. In any case, this takes us back to *Song Offerings* 3 and 70.

3

I know not how thou singest, my master! I ever listen in silent amazement.

The light of thy music illumines the world. The life breath of thy music runs from sky to sky. The holy stream of thy music breaks through all stony obstacles and rushes on.

My heart longs to join in thy song, but vainly struggles for a voice. I would speak, but speech breaks not into song, and I cry out baffled. Ah, thou hast made my heart captive in the endless meshes of thy music, my master!

> 70
> Is it beyond thee to be glad with the gladness of this rhythm? to be tossed and lost and broken in the whirl of this fearful joy?
>
> All things rush on, they stop not, look not behind, no power can hold them back, they rush on.
>
> Keeping steps with that restless, rapid music, seasons come dancing and pass away—colours, tunes and perfumes pour in endless cascades in the abounding joy that scatters and gives up and dies every moment.[1]

Incidentally, these two are instances of why possibly Tagore chose prose rhythms to match the marvel of his verse in the original. They stand on their own feet.

I have been only scratching at the poetry that not only won him the Nobel Prize but gave him the company of world poets. How right Brahmabandhab Upadhyay had been to confer this title on him and anticipate the fame! And I, a century later and a most occasional reader of world poetry, do not seem to tire of saying that Tagore's '*he purna taba charaner kaachhe / jaahaa-kichhu sab aachhe aachhe aachhe* (*Naivedya* 14: 'Thou All Perfect, / everything abides at Thy feet / for all time' in Tagore's own translation [*Poems* 23]) is no less memorable than Dante's much acclaimed 'E'n la sua volontade è nostra pace' (*Paradiso*, III. 85: And in his will is our peace). Or for that matter, Goethe's 'Entbehren sollst du, sollst entbehren' (*Faust*, I, 4: l. 1549: You must give up, must give up [quoted by Tagore himself in *Chinnapatra*, 5 October 1895]): notwithstanding its

1 *The English Writings of Rabindranath Tagore*, ed. Sisir Kumar Das, Vol. 1 (New Delhi: Sahitya Akademi, 1994, rpt. 2004), pp. 43, 67.

different context, does it not fetch us '*aamaar je sab dite habe*' from *Gitimalya* 101?

> I have to give up all, I know.
> All my riches, lord, and all my words.
> My eyes' seeing, my ears' hearing,
> my hands' fine service, and my movements.
> Give up all.
>
> My dawn and dusk lying hidden
> in heart's leaf-cup will bloom out to you.
> That which is my *veena* now, tuning,
> will sound by becoming yours at your scale.
> Give up all.
>
> Filling up with my sorrow and happiness
> your joy you turn mine, and then make it yours.
> When what I have as mine I give back
> as yours, it becomes truly mine.
> Give up all.

2014 (in Occasional Paper – *8, eds. Tapati Mukhopadhyay and Uma Majumdar, Raj Bhavan, Kolkata in collaboration with Visva-Bharati, Santiniketan)*

Tagore's 'Puja' Songs in the Background of 'Bhakti'

A hundred years ago Tagore wrote a song later included in *Gitabitan*, his collection of songs as rearranged by him, under the section 'Puja' (Worship), subsection "Bondhu" (Friend), beginning '*tomaay natun kore paabo bole haaraai kshane-kshan / o mor bhaalobaasaar dhan*', roughly rendered as 'To get you ever anew I go on losing you, / you my love-treasure.' The rest of the song in my tentative English is:

(To get you ever anew I go on losing you,
you my love-treasure.)
Saying you will come you disappear,
my love-treasure.
Oh, you are not hidden from me, you are ever mine—
in a moment's play you are now immersed,
my love-treasure.
When I search for you fear grips me—
and my love surges in a wave.
You have no end, so playing cipher you go on
    ending yourself—

> and my *viraha*'s tears wash that smile of yours,
> Oh my love-treasure.

If we take a close look at the words, we first find a pair of contraries: 'get/'lose' and 'come'/'disappear'. Then there is a synonymous statement at the next stage: 'not hidden'='ever'—which is set against 'a moment's'. The 'fear' in the stage after is the fear of not finding. Now, that is overlapped with 'love surges'; no wonder it does so since love is no less the urge than union. Finally, the 'no end' calls forth its contrary, 'cipher', but its apposite 'playing' turns it around, 'go on ending' being its logical extension. That causes the 'tears' belonging to '*viraha*' (separation) whose contrary, 'smile' is linked back to the 'playing'. But the synaesthetic 'wash' (*my viraha's tears wash that smile of yours*) brings the spoken to 'you', the love-treasure 'you', down to the level of the speaker 'I'—no 'you' if there is no 'I', a perception we come across again and again in the 'Puja' songs—indeed the one that Tagore is going to put forward to Einstein in their celebrated conversation in 1930. Of course we can look deeper, not just in search of traditional tropes, but of the existentialist nature of that *viraha*, so ably explicated some three decades ago by Jagannath Chakraborty (*Gitanjali: Astitva-Viraha* [Kolkata: Ananda Publishers Private Ltd., 1988]).

Let us take another song from the same subsection "Bondhu" (Friend) written about a year before ('*aamaar hiyaar maajhe lukiye chhile, dekhte aami paaini*'):

> You were hidden in my heart, and I didn't see you.
> I looked out, but didn't look in.

In all my loves, in all hurts and hopes
you stood by me, but I didn't seek you.
You were the joy of all my play—
yet overlooking you I had my joy, and days were spent
 in idleness.
Hiding deep in my life you put tunes
to my songs of sorrow and happiness, but I didn't sing
 your song.

This is a simpler text admitting the failure of 'I' to recognise 'you', lacking the subtlety of the first song. But admission to such failure in recognition is another kind of recognition. If we were making a distinction between medieval *bhakti* and Tagore's *puja*, we would perhaps see more *bhakti* in this one, or rather, less *bhakti* in the other. Yet a trope like '*You have no end, so playing cipher you go on ending yourself*' contains more to evince *bhakti* than any of the tropes in its companion.

Let us now take a song from the subsection "Viraha" (Separation)—'*prabhu, tomaa laagi aankhi jaage*':

Lord, for you are my eyes awake;
you I haven't seen
I look out,
that too I enjoy.
Sitting at door's dust, ah the beggar heart
craves your grace;
I get none
only beg it,
that too I enjoy.
In this world how happy and how busy

> people have gone ahead;
> I had no companion,
> you I wait for,
> that too I enjoy.
> All around a honey-filled, eager and green earth
> brings tears of love;
> you I haven't seen
> I am pained,
> that too I enjoy.

The stress on '*that too I enjoy*' brings to light the four acts in the four parts of the song: looking out, begging, waiting, and being pained. Again all four are preceded by a negation (signified by '*nai*' in the original), the first and the last spelt out as the same: '*you I haven't seen*'. But there is a difference in the two circumstances: in the first, the eyes are awake for 'you'; in the last the eyes are full of tears from love of the 'honey-filled, eager and green earth'. This love does render 'you' into a possible perception the absence of which only intensifies the sense of *viraha* or separation. But *viraha* is no less an involvement than *milan* or union. Hence the burden '*that too I enjoy*'.

But *viraha* can be tantamount to an unattained epiphany as in the following song written within a year ('*visva jakhan nidraamagan, gagan andhakaar*'):

> When the world sleeps, and the sky is dark,
> who plucks my *veena*'s strings with such force?
> Snatches sleep from my eyes, and I sit up on bed—
> I peer and gaze, but cannot see him.

In murmur after murmur my mind fills up,
I don't know what mighty words ring so eagerly.
Nor grasp in what sorrow the heart is full of tears,
round whose neck I would put my own garland.

Here 'he' replaces the familiar 'you'. 'He' has come with pronounced enough signs, but 'I' fails to see him. Yet the indirect effects of his arrival are all there: first, a continuous murmur in the mind, evoking some eager and mighty words; then again an undefined sorrow filling up the heart with tears; finally the sense of a could have been union represented by the garland, as it were waiting, to be put around a dear neck.

This may bring us to the subsection "Duhkha" (Sorrow) and to this song in particular—'*aaro aaro prabhu*, *aaro aaro*':

More, more, my Lord, more,
give me more such thrashings.
I have been hiding and fleeing about—
but now I am caught, no escape!
Snatch from me all I have.
And do what is left to be done,
no matter if I lose or you lose.
Being there with people in all places,
laughing and playing I have spent my time—
let me see how you make me cry.

This gets an extra weight when sung by a character in a play that fits the description in the last two lines but one, a *baul* or a *hegemon* of sorts. The psyche of the person is not really that of one '*hiding and fleeing about*'; that is only a way of saying that he had an easier commitment, '*being there with people*'. In other words, he hasn't had the true buffeting of life. The experience implied is that of buffeting. In another "Duhkha" song, written years later, we have a companion feeling in '*aami maarer saagar paari debo bisham jharer baanye / aamaar bhaybhaangaa ei naaye*' ('This thrashing sea I shall steer across with a storm on my trail / in this fear-routing boat of mine.'). In fact this song too is sung by the same character.

But "Duhkha" yields to "Ashvas" (Assurance) as illustrated by '*aachhe duhkha, aachhe mrityu, virahadahan laage*':

> Yes, there is suffering, and death,
>   and separation's scorching.
> Yet there is peace, and joy,
>   and a sense of the endless.
> Yet life flows forever, and the sun,
>   moon and stars smile,
> spring comes to orchards in a variety of colours.
> Waves fall and waves rise,
> flowers shed and flowers bloom.
> There is no decay, no end; no trace of pettiness.
> At that plenitude's feet the heart seeks a place.

This is a well-known 'Puja' song sung often at deaths and memorial meetings. Its pace is slow, tuning us to the rhythm of the endless. The plenitude that is evoked is not extraterrestrial or extra-astral but is the essence of terrestrial cum astral Nature. So there is hardly any traditional *bhakti* in this song—the absence of the familiar 'you' also detracts from it.

I would take the following two songs from the subsection "Bibidha" (Miscellaneous) as paving the way to "Jagaran" (Awakening) and "Ananda" (Joy). First, '*chirasakhaa, chhero naa more chhero naa*':

> O friend forever, do not desert me, do not desert.
> You, undaunted support in the thick of samsara, stay
> by when I am lonely or with people,
> like riches to the poor, lord to the lord-less,
> strength to the weak.
> Give a new lease of life to the palsied,
> oh you ocean of nectar

There is a prayer in it though no supplication. Defining 'you' as the 'friend forever' argues for a familiarity that rules out supplication. However, the imploring tone cannot be missed. Indeed the subject 'I''s need for support is fully communicated. The 'ocean of nectar' strengthens that, complementing the 'you' and the 'friend forever' equation.

The second "Bibidha" 'Puja' song I had in mind is '*charandhvani suni taba, naath, jibantire*':

> I hear your footsteps, Lord, on life's shores
> in what quiet solitude, in what a pleasant breeze.
> In skies stars and planets look on unblinking,
> in heart a thought-stream flows quite slowly.
> My eyes keep gazing like a thirsty bird,
> my hearing I have spread into my heart's depths—
> on what blissful dawn you will rise in my heart,
> and drowning in joy will all sorrow and happiness pass.

Obviously this is no prayer. Nor is there any imploring in it. Things are in order here—what the subject 'I' has to do is keep ready. The epiphany is going to take place; it is only a question of waiting. This waiting is unlike that in Kafka's parable on the Emperor's Message (*Eine Kaiserliche Botschaft*) where the messenger can never reach the humble subject whom, and whom alone, the Emperor has sent a message from his deathbed—never ever ('*Du aber sitzest an deinem Fenster und erträumst sie dir, wenn der Abend kommt*.' ['But you sit at your window when evening falls and dream it to yourself'—trans. Willa and Edwin Muir]).

The "Jagaran" 'Puja' song I would like to quote is a four-line text ('*vimal aanande jaago re*').

> Wake up in pure joy.
> Be drowned in the ocean of nectar.
> Look out to your heart's east
> and see the first perfect ray of light.

This song of awakening is unlike anything that has gone before. The verbs come in an ascending sequence, and establish the cognition of light the seat of which is the heart. Indeed it is the heart where all such epiphanies occur.

As to the subsection "Ananda" (Joy), here is a song from there—'*bipul taranga re, bipul taranga re*':

> What turbulent waves, ah what turbulent waves!
> Bursting up all skies—drowning the past and future,
> bright with light, with life restless, what waves of joy!
> Hence the sun, moon and stars are swinging,

sensation's flow is trembling with thrills,
eager and restlessly the world dances,
the heart-bird chirps.

What we immediately mark is the key to which this song is set. It is not every day that joy is seen as turbulence. Besides, it is joy as such, immanent, not as a gift from 'you', the prime mover in most of the 'Puja' songs. What matters here is the experience and not its episteme. We are not in the neighborhood of *bhakti* nor even perhaps *puja* in any literal sense.

There are a few other subsections in 'Puja' I would like to quote from. From "Visva" (World) to begin with—'*aakaase dui haate prem bilaay o ke*':

Who is it pouring love in the sky with two hands?
That nectar rolls out from world to world.
Trees store it in the green leaves,
the earth holds it on its head.
Flowers wear it on their petals,
birds draw it on their wings.
Children pick it from mothers' breasts,
mothers find it in children's face.
It is lit up in sorrow's flames,
it melts down in a stream of tears.
From a shattered heroic heart
it flows in a deathlike life-force.
In that rhythm of making and unmaking
it goes on dancing in land to land and age to age.

What do we see in the 'Visva'? Rhythm. And what is the mystery of that rhythm? It is love, love all comprehensive—in nature, in human life, in astral bodies. As to where that love comes from, there is only a vague 'he', no definite 'you'. In fact, the question 'who pours' is pushed to the background by what is being poured and how it is being consumed by all. 'Puja' also projects "Sundar" (the Beautiful), as celebrated in the following song—'*ei-je tomaar prem, ogo hridayharan*':

> This is your love then, O thief of heart,
> this golden light dancing on leaves.
> This sweet leisured way clouds floating in sky,
> this breeze sprinkling nectar on the body.
> Morning light's shower has bathed my eyes.
> Your words of love have thus reached my life.
> There, your face has bent down, putting eyes on mine,
> my heart has today touched your feet.

In the preceding song the stress was on the all-embracing love; here the stress is on the giver of that love. The last but one line is quite physically charged, whether or not tracing any memory of the *Vaishnava Padavali*. Besides, the subject 'I''s feminine persona is clear which may be true of many other 'I'-'you' songs.

'*o aamaar man, jakhan jaagli naa re*' is a song from the subsection "Baul". As I would render it, the text is:

> O my heart, when you were not woken
> your soul's darling came to the door.
> Hearing him going away your sleep snapped—

> oh your sleep snapped in the dark.
> Spreading the end of my saree on ground I spend the
> night alone.
> His flute plays in darkness; my eyes do not see him.
> Tell me, how can eyes find him whom you did not heed?
> Now can you get him by roaming the road whom you
> did not let in?

I am not sure if the 'soul's darling' at all carries the sense of '*maner maanush*' which is a key concept of *baul* thought. There is another partial rendering in the 'heart' for '*man*' in the very first line, especially since it is '*man*' that was not awake when the '*maner maanush*' came. In other words, the state of being unawake has more significance than it appears in my English. Such are the pitfalls of translation, but perhaps an admission to the lapses bails out the translator to a degree. Anyway, the story contained in the song is not utterly unfamiliar to Tagore's audience.

From the subsection "Path" (Way) let me take '*asrunadir sudur paarey ghaat dekhaa jaay tomaar dvaare*'. The text is:

> On the distant shore of the river of tears is seen the
> quay at your door.
> Bound at my own hand half inside home and
> half outside—
> let me go sailing now in the evening breeze.
> My time was spent on the market day
> by buying the burden of people's words.
> Put down that weight of words, heart, and go quiet
> and hear, oh hear

what song rings out to *veena*'s strings
    in the shore breeze.

A key phrase here is 'bound at my own hand' attended upon by the graphic 'half inside home and half outside'. The subject 'I' has to win over that ambivalence. Another key is in 'the burden of people's words' which comes in the way of paying heed to the distant song. Only by putting that burden down can the way be attained.

Let me close this narration of Tagore's 'Puja' songs with an instance from the subsection "Sesh" (End)—'*sesh naahi je, sesh kathaa ke bolbe*':

There is no end, so who can say the last word?
It all came as a blow, it will burst into flames.
When clouds have their day rains will begin to pour,
after snow is all frozen it will melt into rivers.
What finishes only looks to finish,
on crossing doors of darkness it gets to light.
Breaking the mould of the old the new will bloom out,
after life has blossomed death will bear the fruit.

The opening is like the Rigvedic Nāsadīya Sūkta reversed. Since there is no apocalypse, there cannot be any 'Revelation'. There is a cosmology implied in the second line; but it surely is not the Big Bang (the song predates Georges Lemaître by thirteen years), though the images of 'blow' and 'fire' are close enough. It is probably derived from the Upanishads on how the 'Brahmāṇḍa' came to be. And there may be a hint in the last lines of the ancient *Purāṇic* notion of 'Kalpāntara'. Besides, it evokes the memory of the master trope from the very first 'Puja' song I quoted, '*tomaar sesh naahi, tai sunya seje sesh kare daao aapnaake je*' ('You have no end, so playing cipher you go on ending yourself'), thus bringing the first part of my discourse full circle. My apologies, however, for quoting only fifteen, and referring to one in passing, out of 626 songs marked 'Puja' by Tagore himself.

We know that Tagore was not an idol worshipper. So his *puja* cannot mean idol worship, let alone worship by priestly mediation. His '*prabhu*' or '*nath*' ('lord' in the rendering here) whom he often invokes is no deity in the common sense of the term. *Bhakti* defied traditional worship by defying the priestly mediation, but it did have a deity in purview, whether *saguna*, with attributes, or *nirguna*, without attributes. In other words, *bhakti*'s mien is personal, and can be only partially institutionalised in the *bhaktas*' togetherness, not ritualistically though. Kabir and Nanak, Tagore's favourites among medieval *sant* poets, shunned institutionalised worship. And Mira, whom Tagore quotes as Kumudini's ideal in the novel *Jogajog* (Relations), was only loyal to her '*giridhari nagara*'. As to Tukaram some of whose poems had been translated by Tagore in his early youth, Vithova or Vitthal was the frame of reference. One such translation is of the *abhang* beginning '*nāmdeveñ keleñ svapnāmājī jāgeñ / sabeñ pāndarange jeuniāñ//*', recently rendered into English by Dilip Chitre:

I was only dreaming
Namdeo and Vitthal
Stepped into my dream

"Your job is to make poems,"
said Namdeo,
"Stop fooling around."

Vitthal gave me the measure
And slapped me gently
To arouse me
From my dream
Within a dream

"The grand total
Of the poems Namdeo vowed to write
Was one billion,"
He said,
"All the unwritten ones, Tuka,
Are your dues."[1]

There is a subsection in 'Puja' named "Prarthana" (Prayer) containing thirty-six songs. Of them only a few are straight prayers, '*padapraante raakho sebake*' ('Keep your servant at your feet') being the most obvious one. Even that is not addressed to a 'you' belonging to a pantheon; we are only told of a '*devadeva*', 'god of gods', who has a whole host to bestow. This 'prayer' sounds quite formal, almost ceremonial, beside the urgency of '*andhajane deho aalo, mritajane deho praan*'

1 *Says Tuka*-1 (Pune: Sonheimer Cultural Association, 2003), p. 3.

('Give light to the blind, give life to the dead') which Tagore was once in late life heard humming to himself on bed at night, or of '*jiban jakhan sukaaye jaay karunaadhaaraay eso*' ('When the heart is hard and parched up, come upon me with a shower of mercy' [Tagore's own rendering]), the song, as said above, Tagore had sung to Gandhi at his break of a crucial fast at Pune's Yarveda jail. Besides, the distance between the 'I' and the 'you'—the prayee and the prayed to—is in most cases minimised, with the ultimate hope: 'With more love from you, more love / let my "I" be drowned.' The theme of 'you'-'I' that seems to hold the key to the 'Puja' songs in general is no less pronounced in these non-ceremonial 'prayers'. It would be interesting to see how Tagore reaches his 'Puja' "Prarthana" from the early *brahmasamgit*s some of which may look a little stiff ('Seated on your huge throne, O father of the worlds, / you are listening to the song of the universe made from your own rhythm', for instance), but some rather supple, such as 'With great hopes I have come, Oh, call me to your side, / do not send me back, Mother' or 'At your door I am, Lord, all day—my eyes fill up with tears'. His familiar 'you' hasn't quite come to shape yet in those songs—he is mostly invoking powers that motivate life. They are often called 'Father' with the familial analogy not ruled out. They are also called 'Lord' not without a hint of the status. Sometimes they are called 'Mother' to suggest the needed affection. There are also a few instances of 'Friend' ('Darling friend has come today—look, world, look'). Can we call these early *brahmasamgit*s instances of *bhakti*? True, they do not have the intensity we have in Andal or Akka Mahadevi or Mira or Lal, or Ramprasad nearer home, yet they are words of devotion. They imply a Presence. Now, to what extent by the same token can we ascribe *bhakti to* Tagore's "Prarthana" songs in the 'Puja' section?

Is this my cue to recall, with all trepidations of a fringe audience, Srimanta Sankaradeva's *Bargit*s which are medieval *bhakti* on its heights? Of the thirty-four or thirty-five extant, I have five of them in mind: '*paave pari hari karoha kaatari / praana raakhabi mora / bishay bishadhara / bishe jara jara / jivana naarahe thora*'; '*gopaale ki gati kaile / govinde ki mati dile / naatha biphale janama saba gela re*'; '*mana meri raama charanahi laagu / toi dekhotaa antaka aagu*'; '*naaraayana kaahe bhakati karo teraa / meri pamaraa mana mudhava ghaneghana / ghaatuka paapa naachorh*'; '*soi soi thaakura moi yo hari parakaashaa / naama smarata, rupa dharata, taakeri haamu daasaa*'. All five have been rendered into English by various hands. Based on them, and often lifting entire phrases from them, I may try afresh.

(a)

I fall at your feet, Hari, and beg with tears,
do save my life.
Possessions are a serpent spreading poison in me
beyond endurance.

Men and money are fickle, fickle life and youth,
fickle this samsara too.
Sons and wife are of no worth,
then whom to value?

Like water on a lotus leaf is my mind, restless,
cannot even hold a moment.
World it doesn't fear, only gluts, O Lord,
skirting your blissful feet.
Sankara says, O Hrishikesa, take me across
this ocean of sorrow.
Śri's consort, you are my goal, my soul, give
thought, path, instructions.

(b)
What path did Gopala show,
what disposition did Govinda give?
Alas, Lord, my days are all gone in vain.

This world is a dense forest struck up with delusions,
there we move about as deer—
catching us in maya's traps the time hunter
comes rushing
and the dogs of lust and rage keep chasing and biting.
We lose our senses, Hari, and don't know how escape,
in sin is our life charred.
Greed and delusion are two tigers to never let us go—
protect us, O good Lord—
there is no running away, we are ever worse prisoners,
with the mind losing its grip.
You, Hari, to your feet I pray, lift this veil of maya,
Sankara keeps imploring you.

(c)
O my mind, you better lie at Rama's feet;

don't you see the end approaching?

Mind, the life-span is every moment shortened;
look, any day the breath may slip away.
Mind, when the time python swallows up,
you know that death occurs on the instant?
Mind, the body is sure to collapse;
so worship Rama leaving illusions.
O my mind, you are vain with your possessions,
why seeing that you do not see, you blind one?
Mind, why do you sleep over your pleasures?
Wake up, and contemplate Govinda.
Mind, with knowledge does Sankara say,
see, there is no refuge but Rama.

(d)
Narayana, how can I be devoted to you?
My sinful mind, O Madhava, doesn't stop
doing violence again and again.

All moving creatures, worms and flies, and all unmoving,
trees and hills, are your body.
I kill them all to fill up my belly
without showing these creatures any pity.
In Īśa-form, Hari, you sit in all pitchers
as though you are pervading the whole sky.
It is abuse, railing and violence, Hari,
we deal out to you, we sinners.
Sankara begs, be kind to him, Lord,
so that he doesn't give up the word Rama.

Your name will do away with sins,
so knowing I seek refuge in it.

(e)
They alone are my lord who manifest Hari,
bearing his name and form; only him I serve.

The scholar merely reads scriptures,
the devotee takes their essence;
the lotus blooms with water inside,
the bee drinks its honey.
Liberation is where devotion is,
this the devotee knows,
as the merchant knows the value
of the philosopher's stone.
Krishna's servant, Sankara says,
worship Govinda's feet;
he is the true scholar, truly bejewelled,
who sings Hari's glory.

If we scan these five songs, what do we find? To begin with, what do the 'dhrums' or *asthayi*s tell us? As to the *abhogas* we are sure that there will be a prayer bearing the poet's signature. But it is the *asthayi* that must lead us through the *antara* and the *sanchari* to that prayer. In the first song ('*paave pari hari karoha kaatari*') the theme is possessions' poison; in the second ('*gopaale ki gati kaile*'), it is days gone in vain; in the third ('*mana meri raama charanahi laagu*'), the stress is on death; in the fourth ('*naaraayana kaahe bhakati karo teraa*'), it is on sin; and in the fifth ('*soi soi thaakura moi yo* *hari parakaasaa*') on devotion as such. From possessions' poison comes the issue of impermanence of money, men, life and youth. We also have a distant echo of the other Sankara's *Mohamudgara*. Opposed to that is worldliness cum '*bhoga*' resulting in a reluctance to salvage. Hence the prayer, to Śri's consort (an echo of Ramanuja's 'Śri-Vaishnavism?), not just to help cross the 'ocean of sorrow' but for '*tattva pantha upadesa*', three crucial words, perhaps revealing Sankaradeva's Neo-Vaishnavite agenda.

In the *antara* and the *sanchari* of the second song an image is built up of deer being, one, trapped by the time hunter ('*kaala vyaadha*'), two, chased and bitten by the dogs of lust and rage, and, three, followed by greed and delusion in the shape of two tigers. The hunter, the dogs and the tigers are part of the dense forest that the world is. It is indeed a prison house from which the deliverance can only come through a prayer which is uttered by the poet. While time is here a hunter, in the third song it is a python ('*ajagara*') that is given to swallowing, a metaphor apt enough in the context of death ('*antaka*') which is the basic theme of the song. There is something special about this song in that it is an exhortation to the mind ('*mana*') with the word leading every third line. This adds to the intensity of the song, the last line's perception ('there is no refuge but Rama') bearing out the first line's exhortation.

The fourth song is the song of sin and violence chiefly consisting in our eating up of nature. One may wonder, just wonder, if there has been a shadow of Jainism cast here. Surely Gandhi would have been happy if he had known this song. However, with equal assurance it may be said that Darwin would have flown in the face of it if he had any knowledge of such sentiments. Does the song also presuppose some knowledge of Īśopanishad in '*īśa-svarupe hari saba ghate baithaha*', or is that a reflection of the '*ghata-pata*' debate of the Nyāya ('*yoicana gagana viyaapi*')? Along with the usual signature the *abhoga* in this song also carries a hint of '*ekasarana naama dharma*' in '*tuwaa naama*' and '*taahe sarana lehu*'.

The fifth song is built around the very devotion that Sankaradeva is preaching. There is a contrast between the traditional scholar reading *sastra*s and the devotee. As *jnana* is inferior to *bhakti*, the *sastra*s' essence is not revealed to the scholar, but to the devotee. There is a metaphor used to bring this home: the honey inside the blooming lotus doesn't give it anything, but that honey is drunk by the bee. What is more, the devotee knows that in devotion lies liberation, as the merchant knows—so goes the simile used in this connection—the value of the rarest of the rare stones [so to speak, the philosopher's stone]. This philosophy of devotion might have been drawn on *Bhagavadgītā*'s thirteenth 'adhyāya', the 'Bhaktiyoga'. But it may also have come from the *Bhāgavata-purāṇa* and be taken as a preamble in spirit to Sankaradeva's treatise on *Bhakti-ratnākara*, culled, as we know, from the *Bhāgavata-purāṇa* and some of its analogous sources as well as commentaries.

It is obvious that Sankaradeva's *bhakti*, as seen from these *Bargit*s, and Tagore's 'Puja' are quite dissimilar. We have a 'you' in Sankaradeva too, except in the third song which is a straight 'ramaini', to use the Kabir-related terminology, but that 'you' is 'Hari'. Sankaradeva is too religiously motivated to admit any ambiguity—*bhakti* is the corner stone of the neo-Vaishnavism he is preaching. The song I failed to render into English, '*jaya jaya jaadava jalanidhijaadhava dhaataa / srutamaatraakhilatraataa / smarane karaya siddhi dinadayaanidhi / bhukuti-mukutipadadaataa*' lists his God's attributes that only justify the *bhakti* He is offered. Its religious connotation cannot be overlooked.

Is Tagore's 'Puja' then less distant from Kabir's *bhakti* whom after all he has translated with Evelyn Underhill's assistance? Did he feel an affinity with him, for the *One Hundred Poems of Kabir*, we know, almost came in the heels of his English *Gitanjali* a good many of which poems in their Bengali original were part of 'Puja'? Here is the very first of his Kabir, '*Mo ko kahan dhunro bande*':

> O servant, where dost thou seek Me?
> Lo, I am beside thee.
> I am neither in temple nor in mosque: I am neither in Kaaba nor in Kailash:
> Neither am I in rites and ceremonies, nor in yoga and renunciation.
> If thou art a true seeker, thou shalt at once see Me: thou shalt meet Me in a moment of time.
> Kabir says, 'O Sadhu! God is the breath of all breath.'

In the same vein are a number of songs, for instance this short one ('*pani vic min piyasi*'):

> I laugh when I hear that the fish in the water is thirsty:

> You do not see that the Real is in your home, and you wander
> from forest to forest listlessly!
> Here is the truth! Go where you will, to Benares or to Mathura;
> if you do not find your soul, the world is unreal to you.

Tagore would probably appreciate the *nirguna* thrust of these songs, but would not use the same or similar *saguna* register hinted in them. One reason why he would not is of course he belonged to an altogether different time. Besides, there is the question of upbringing and of sensibility peculiar to him. Curiously, he had almost nothing to do with Ramakrishna whose Kali must have left him cold. He knew Ramprasad, but more perhaps for his music than his *bhakti* which was fully *saguna*. One of his influences, we know, was from Vaishnava Padavali, but it is doubtful if he had any regard for Vaishnava faith as practised in his time, though his respectful portrayal of a mendicant Vaishnava woman is unforgettable. He knew that *saguna* registers were still active, especially in villages where religion was part of everyday life; but if he would ever sing *bhakti* it would be *nirguna*. Another Kabir from his translations is '*sadho, sahajai kaya shodho*' which brings out the philosophy of *nirguna* to the full:

> O sadhu! purify your body in the simple way.
>
> As the seed is within the banyan tree, and within the seed are the flowers, the fruits, and the shade:
>
> So the germ is within the body, and within that germ is the body again.
>
> The fire, the air, the water, the earth, and the aether; you cannot have these outside of Him.

> O Kazi, O Pundit, consider it well: what is there that is not in the soul?
>
> The water-filled pitcher is placed upon water, it has water within and without.
>
> It should not be given a name, lest it call forth the error of dualism.
>
> Kabir says, 'Listen to the Word, the Truth, which is your essence. He speaks the Word to Himself; and He Himself is the Creator.'

It is a rich text, one of the richest in Tagore's Kabir translations. The short Kabir song '*mor phakirwaa maangi jaay*',

> The Beggar goes a-begging, but I could not even catch sight of Him:
> And what shall I beg of the Beggar? He gives without my asking.
> Kabir says: 'I am His own: now let befall what may befall!'

may remind us of its reverse in Tagore's song from the "Bondhu" subsection in 'Puja': '*ere bhikhaari saajaaye ki ranga tumi karile, / haasite aakaas bharile*':

> Oh, the jests you had by making him a beggar!
> You filled up the skies with laughter.
> He went about in streets, from door to door, and put
> what he got inside his sack—
> but ah, you came ever so often and snatched away his
> begged-up treasure.
> He thought he was ever a destitute on earth, a
> destitute to life, to death.

> But you king of kings, when in great fear at day's end
>   he came to your home—
> you offered him half your seat and put your own
>   garland around him.

The drama is here elaborate, not as curt as in the Kabir song. Is the difference in the straightness of faith; or in the space around the 'you' in Tagore and its relative lack around the 'He' in Kabir? This latter is worth pursuing whether or not we arrive thereof at the relative character of the faith. Is Tagore writing a modern version of *bhakti*? In other words, if we translate him back into the 15th century idiom, will we arrive at a variation on Kabir? There is a fondness around this query; maybe it is better to look into Tagore's 'Puja' in its own terms and not propose it as a modern version of Kabir's *nirguna*. Besides Kabir's being a Sant and having initiated a *Panth* makes a difference. That 'sakhi' in the *Bijaka* where Kabir's home is said to be on top, its path being so sharp and slippery that even ants slip, no question of any person going there with a loaded ox ('*kabir kaa ghar sikhar par, / jahaan silhali gaila. / paanv na tikai papilakaa, / tahan khalkan laadai baila*') may indeed be loaded with contemporary mysticism.

Does Nanak make a difference? Is his *nirguna* anywhere nearer? Tagore's visit to Amritsar with his father at eleven on their way to Dalhousie, and stay there for a month listening to Sikh *bhajans* at the Golden Temple, left a mark on him. He has a vivid memory of that in his *Jibansmriti* (*My Reminiscences*) written at the age of fifty. Besides, one of the 'Puja' songs from the subsection "Ananda" is developed from his translation of a Sikh bhajan, '*baaje baaje ramyabinaa baaje*' (At play, the lovely *veena* is at play) < '*Baadoi baadoi ramyabinaa baadoi*'. He was also familiar with the famous 'Sabad' of Nanak's which had been earlier collected by his father and in all probability translated by him: '*gagan mai thaalu ravi-candu dipak bane*' ('*gaganer thaale ravi chandra dipak jvale*'). Tagore has also written on Nanak with the highest regard for his message of universal love.

Here are three instances of Nanak Bani, as translated by Harjeet Singh Gill, which will perhaps give us an idea of how Nanak's bhakti is different from Tagore's 'Puja'.

(a)
some call me a ghost
others address me as a madman
some refer to my innocence
others recall my ignorance

yes, Nanak is mad
mad in love with the Lord of the universe
mad in love with the Sovereign of the divine kingdom

he exists only for his Love
he lives only for his Lord
he breathes in His presence
he vibrates with His omniscience

in this madness, there is no pride, no pretence
in this madness there is joy, there is presence
there is love, there is benevolence!

(b)
blessed is the paper
and blessed are the pen and inscription
Nanak, blessed is the scribe
who dictates the discourse of divine reflection!

(c)
where does one come from?
where does one go?
where does one stay steady and serene?

with the grace of the Guru
the devotee sheds greed and lust
with the grace of the Guru
he gains His trust

how does one arrive at His perception?
how does one follow His projection?
Nanak, please enlighten us with this sublime reflection

in His will is birth
in His will is death
in His will is every breath
with the word of the Guru
the devotee perceives His truth
with the word of the Guru
he stays in His divine refuge![2]

2 Harjeet Singh Gill, trans. *Nānak Bāṇī*, Vol. II (Patiala: Punjabi University, 2007), pp. 855, 1177, 786 respectively.

That, in spite of his great admiration for Kabir and Nanak, Tagore's 'Puja' is not like their *bhakti* need not be a matter of discouragement to us, for to call Tagore a modern-day Kabir and Nanak will indeed be going wide of the mark. True, the word 'Puja' is a little misleading; taken in isolation it may sound a variation on *bhakti*. But we would do better not to take it in isolation. When he was rearranging the *Gitabitan*, he wrote the following note:

> When the *Gitabitan* was first published its compilers were in too much of a hurry to put a thematic order among the songs. Not only has that been an impediment to its use, but has also done harm to literary relish. Therefore, in this edition the songs have been arranged in order of their themes. In this way, even without help from tunes, the readers may be able to follow the songs as lyric.

His thematic divisions are six-fold: 'Puja' (Worship), 'Svadesh' (Homeland), 'Prem' (Love), 'Prakriti' (Nature), 'Bichitra' (Various), 'Anushthanik' (Formal-Ritual). 'Puja' has the largest number of songs, spread over twenty-one subsections. The second largest is 'Prem' with two subsections, third 'Prakriti' with seven subsections, fourth 'Bichitra', fifth 'Svadesh'; the sixth and the smallest is 'Anushthanik'. In other words, 'Puja' is put in perspective: 'Puja' is not what the others are, especially, 'Prem' which may veer to it. If in these two sections, the bulk of Tagore's songs are an interplay of 'I' and 'you'—the 'I' speaking and the 'you' spoken to, then perhaps the 'I' predominates in 'Prem' and the 'you' in 'Puja'. What is 'Prem' if not the 'I's' urge to 'you', and what is 'Puja' if not the 'you' being sought by 'I'?

The twenty-one subsections of 'Puja' are: "Gaan" (Songs), "Bondhu" (Friend), "Praarthana" (Prayer), "Viraha" (Separation), "Sadhana o Samkalpa" (Seeking and Resolution), "Duhkha" (Sorrow), "Ashvas" (Assurance), "Antarmukhe" (Inwardly), "Atmabodhan" (Self-appearance), "Jagaran" (Awakening), "Nihsamshay" (Doubtlessness), "Sadhak" (Seeker), "Utsab" (Festivity), "Ananda" (Joy), "Visva" (World), "Bibidha" (Miscellany), "Sundar" (the Beautiful),"'Baul" (Mendicant Singer), "Path" (Way), "Sesh" (End), "Parinay" (Wedding). Of these the last subsection has a little formality about it, in its invocation to the lord to motivate the newlywed couple to fulfil their vow, or in its counsel to that very couple to be ever steered by the lord. There may be an occasional formality in some of the other subsections too, with a hint perhaps of his former *brahmasamgit* catching up with him. But I am not speaking of a song like '*nibhrita praaner devataa jekhaane jaagen ekaa*' from the smallest subsection, "Saadhak":

Where the god of the lonely hearts wakes alone,
oh devotee, open that door—I shall get to him today.
Out all day and roaming about, whom do I look for,
I haven't yet learnt to offer the evening *arati*.
By lighting my life's flame from your lit-up life
oh worshipper, I'll remotely put together my offering.
Where from all world's devotion comes
 the glow of worship
there I too shall hold a ray of light.

It is intensely felt. Such intensity of feeling is hard to rationalise in purely material terms. Perhaps it marks one end of 'Puja' the other being a song like '*tomaay notun kore paabo bole haaraai kshane-kshan*'. In other words, I am thinking of a range or of a number of nodes between these two ends. At which node would then the song, for instance, '*gabhir rajani naamila hridaye, aar kolaahal naai*' from the subsection "Antarmukhe" be placed? In translation the text is:

> A deep night descends on heart, no more any noise.
> From time to time I only hear the distant sea.
> All desire is called back, and outside a dense dark
> thickens—while
> inside the lonely heart a lamp burns without flicker.
> In unending goodness sinks grace,
> the conflict resolves.
> The light-hearted and restless play of waves terminates
> in ocean.
> In a silent chant in the heart, rings peace, ah peace,
> seeing unearthly beauty inside I gaze on with
> closed eyes.

It doesn't say in so many words what that 'unearthly beauty' consists of. Besides, there is no intensity of feeling here. Almost inadvertently the ringing of peace (let us not overlook the synaesthesia) is recorded. In the original the word '*saanti*' is thrice repeated though without creating any tremor. With the initial perception of a deep night descending on the heart with all noises abated and with a thick spread of darkness outside, we are invited to a quiet drama (a variation on the dark night of the soul?). We are told of a lamp, no matter how thin, burning, and burning steadily—a hint that some finer perception is going to take place. It does, in two steps. The first step is the perception of a conflict resolution, the conflict of grace or beauty and good—a major resolution for a poet whose primary involvement is with beauty (we may be reminded of a line from another 'Puja' song, from the subsection "Prarthana", '*ei-je dharani cheye bose aachhe ihaar maadhuri baaraao he*' [Give more grace to this earth that is looking upward for love]). The second step is the perception that light-heartedness and restlessness do end. It is not a god-song as the one above and there is no question of worship in it. Yet the closed eyes' gazing at the inward infinite is a rare experience. It is *abhog* in more than one sense.

It is in perfect order in Tagore's world of songs that 'Puja' should begin with a subsection on "Gaan". In our search for the variety of nodes between the two extremes of 'Puja' we may look up a song from it. Let me take '*kanthe nilem gaan, aamaar sesh paaraanir kari*':

> I loaded my voice with song, my last ferry's coin—
> I won't stay behind on the quay alone.
> My song-relishing boatman
> I shall charm away by singing,
> so hoping I get on to the ferry.
> Who knows if I will cross or not cross—
> yet distant winds have called this mad singer.
> O you darlings, you worry for nothing,
> I shall go, I shall, go—
> the door breaks down, and the ropes are snapped.

There is not even the familiar 'you' in this song, let alone 'he' or a cognate (except perhaps a link in the 'boatman'): maybe we should put it, instead of '*tomaay natun kore paabo bole*' at the opposite end of '*nibhrita praaner devataa*' in 'Puja's' scale. This is a song about crossing or death and about its acceptance, not resignation to it. For the 'song' to be the last ferry's coin is giving it a value beyond life, as if it is a bridge to death. In other words, the 'song' belongs as much to death as to life, as attested by the image of the 'song-relishing boatman'. Is charming him the first step to charm the other shore? In another song from this subsection we have it borne out, no matter in how different a context: '*When my days will be over, / when the night will be dark, / song stars will sparkle out in my heart in row after row.*'

Looking through the whole corpus of Tagore's 'Puja' songs, the twenty-one subsections that is, one finds that about one-third are not addressed to a 'you', being songs about 'I' often concerned with a 'he'. Again, of the two-thirds that are addressed to a 'you' a good number are devotional. We may not designate them as *bhakti* in the medieval sense, but their tone of devotion cannot be missed. In fact a few of them could have been sung as *brahmasamgit*, whether or not written to be so. How, for instance, do we take such texts as the following?

(a)

The eager heart goes wandering away—
call it, Lord, to your home
across the world by the nectar-ocean's shore.

(b)

Alas, my thirst is not quenched, not quenched.
Having drunk poison with a paralysed heart
I beg you with folded hands,
cool this samsara-burn in your love's nectar.

(c)

Without you my days are spent, O Lord,
alas, without you my dreams and wakening—
when will you come to my heart?

(d)

If I rush in a restless way like storm-clouds
then take mercy on me, God, take mercy on me.
O you beyond sin, I a destitute have come to
  sin's shore—
take mercy on me, Lord, take mercy, and lift me up.
I live amidst water, yet die of thirst—
take mercy on me, Lord, take mercy and fill up my
  heart with nectar.

Surely they are not as sensitive as their neighbour from the same subsection, "Bibidha" (Miscellany), '*naath he, premapathe sab baadhaa bhaangiyaa daao*':

O Lord, break all obstructions to love's path.
Keep nothing in between, nothing—
and do not stay far, do not.
Alone and with people, at heart and outside
I must ever see you.

If by an oversight Tagore had put this song under 'Prem', the vocative '*naath he*' would have pulled it back to 'Puja'. But if the vocative were not there, would we pull it to 'Prem' or still keep it under 'Puja'? This indeed is a decisive question, for though there are enough devotional markers to define 'Puja', their absence is in no way a detriment to it. We have ample pure 'you' songs, that is, songs without those markers, yet carrying a lot of charge. I just heard a moving singing of '*nayan tomaare paay naa dekhite, rayechha nayane nayane*' (The eyes cannot see you, you stay within eyes), from the same subsection as '*naath he premapathe*'. Its last line reasserts the thrust of the earlier song: '*You and I with none between us, no obstruction from the world.*' The only devotional marker, if at all, may be located in the last but one line: '*I know I will ever have you in world after world in age after age.*'

There may be similarly veiled devotional markers in many of the other, otherwise pure 'you' songs. But there *are* 'you' songs that are thoroughly pure and our concern at the moment is with them. For without coming to terms with them, we cannot fully understand Tagore's *puja*. The identity of 'you' has been variously approached, as the object of 'I''s love or of devotion, or as the inner 'I' or a non-'I' or a greater 'I' that will liberate everyday 'I' of its ego. Early in the day Tagore's faith was not doubted. His roots in the Upanishads were too obvious to be denied. Īśa was said to be a theme to him along with nature, love and man. His poetic career was studied as a measure of their development, in either isolation or in clusters. One such cluster was love and God, or rather love yielding to God. It was not said that he had found God. On the contrary it was said that he was on his way to God. A metaphor of wakefulness and waiting was also put forward. This came to be questioned. Tagore was said to be too much in love with nature and man to believe in an extra-terrestrial power of such dimension. That would involve him in a contradiction in terms. This was not quite an argument between believers and non-believers, or immaterialists and materialists, but between lovers of poetry for its own sake and those for the sake of ideas it carries.

A rapprochement is sometimes sought giving both poetry and philosophy their due. One of Tagore's favourite words from the Upanishads is '*apāvṛṇu*', take the lid off and find out the truth. And a Upanishadic phrase he quotes again and again is '*mā gṛdhaḥ*', do not be greedy. If we take the second to be meant for 'I', then the first may take us to 'you'. Now, what is the truth to Tagore—the rhythm that holds everything together, terrestrial and astral, the rhythm that holds together life and death. If that be so, then 'Puja''s 'you' is worth every attention, call it devotion or not. If, however, our concern is confined to 'I', that is, we go on dissecting the maladies that eventually issue from greed then we may not have any taste left for 'you'. In other words, 'you' may become superfluous, a cliché. But is that within the scope of Tagore's 'Puja' songs that were composed all along his career?

If one takes a comprehensive look at the dates of their composition, one is astounded. We have the first compositions in 1881, a couple to begin with, picking up in the mid- and late 1880s; the pace continued in the mid- and late 1890s, not slackened with the turn of the century. Indeed an even keel was maintained with a thrust at the end of the first decade, reaching the zenith as it were in the middle of the second—one year in the Bengali calendar yielding some 80 songs—the crop going steady into the third decade with quite a few in certain years; some even in the fourth decade, the last date being 1938. From 1881 to 1938 we come across only a few years, six in fact, when no 'Puja' song was composed. So to equate (keeping perhaps in mind the 'Song Offerings' of the English *Gitanjali*) 'Puja' with the *Gitanjali* cycle of poems, meaning *Gitanjali-Gitimalya-Gitali*, is probably not right though it might have marked one of its heights. The song with which I began, '*tomaay natun kore paabo bole haaraai kshane-kshan*' (To get you ever anew I go on losing you), is post-*Gitali*. And one of my later quotes, '*kanthe nilem gaan, aamaar sesh paaraanir kari*' (I loaded my voice with song, my last ferry's coin) is dated 1924. *Puja* has indeed been one of Tagore's lifelong themes.

Puja is not merely seen as 'I''s urge to 'you', but also as 'you''s urge to 'I'. There is a song in the subsection "Nihsamshay" (Doubtlessness) that spells it out, '*taai tomaar aananda aamaar 'par / tumi taai esechho niche*':

> In me is your joy and so
> you have come down—
> without me, O Lord of three worlds,
> your love would have no meaning.
> For me you have this spread of plenty,
> relish pours through my heart,
> taking all these shapes in my life
> your desire is rolling down like a wave.

> Thus, though a king of kings
> to get hold of my heart
> you are going about in charming shapes,
> keeping all awake, O Lord.
> Hence, Lord, where descended
> your love it is that the devotee feels
> and there with the two in union is plenitude found.

It would be too facile to call it Vaishnava *lila* and leave it there. On the other hand, we may try to understand his dialogue with Einstein in the light of these words. The universe is not self-sufficient; it needs a viewer the absence of whom is tantamount to the absence of the universe. In other words, there is no 'you' if there is no 'I'. We would surely recall Einstein's comment on Tagore's relativism, 'then, I am more religious than you.' If religion means 'you' without 'I', then Tagore is perhaps less religious. But given the 'I' the resplendence of the 'you' is not doubted by him. The song we quoted is dated 1910, his *annus mirabilis* in a way, but let me quote a song from twenty-three years later where too we have the same experience, though somewhat more innocuously put forward and with the 'you' turned into a 'he'. It is from the subsection "Baul".

> It is him I know, him who knows me for his own—
> to his gifts I have claims whose rights are over mine.
> Who recognises me and him I recognise in view
>   of that—
> the same light of recognition we have, in his heart
>   and in mine.
> Those who took cover in their own darkness

among them I was bereft of my own self.
He touched me with the golden wand and the sleep's
    cover was burst—
and my eyes rushed to his lit-up face.

Perhaps this is what characterises Tagore's *puja* irrespective of whether the devotional markers are there. We have a duality, an 'I' and 'you' or an 'I' and 'he', in perfect amity. This does not amount to *bhakti* where the one tends to merge with the other. True, there had been various modes of *bhakti*, and of different religious cum theological leanings, but all were God-struck. There might not have been the kind of 'madness' that was seen, for instance, in Vasavanna, the father of Kannad 'Virasaivism', and I am quoting from Sisir Kumar Das' article on 'The Mad Lover', included in the book of that name (Papyrus: Kolkata, 1984), tracing the madness inherent in much *bhakti*:

Feet will dance
eyes will see
tongue will sing
and not find content.
What else, what else
shall I do?

I worship with my hands,
the heart is not content.
What else shall I do?

Listen my lord,
It isn't enough.

I have it in me
to cleave thy belly
and enter thee
O lord of the meeting rivers.
(trans. A. K. Ramanujan, *Speaking of Siva*, Penguin. 1973)

Madness apart, such thirst for God was common to all *bhakti*. Indeed the story of *bhakti* is the story of this thirst in all its ramifications which included the levelling of creed, caste and gender. *Bhakti* is not mere worship; *bhakti* is a state of mind. The closest Tagore's *puja* could get to *bhakti* is perhaps in that song of worship where 'the god of the lonely hearts' is to be given offerings. The word *bhakta* is used there in the sense of a worshipper, an exemplar so to speak in such worship. The word also occurs in the last but one line of the song quoted above, '*taai tomaar aananda aamaar 'par'* (In me is your joy), '*bhaktapraan'*, rendered simply as 'devotee' devoid of any extra charge involving *bhakti*. Going by the *Gītā*, one of its sources, *bhakti* is a yoga, a *marga* like *jñāna*, karma and *dhyāna*. Tagore's 'puja', even in the sense of worship, is much short of that.

Now, since Tagore has written so many 'Puja' songs throughout his creative career, he does not necessarily invite comparison with *bhakti* poets, with Kabir and Nanak, Sankaradeva of whom he had unfortunately no knowledge, with Mira, with Chandidas and Vidyapati (the Vaishnava *brajabuli* he had tried to reproduce very early in the day in the Chatterton fashion creating the near spoof, *Bhanusimha Thakurer Padavali*), with Tukaram some of whose *abhang*s he had translated, let alone the Tamil Nayanmars and Alwars as well as the Kannad Vacanakaras whom he did not know. Apropos Sankaradeva's *Bargit*s, Upendranath Sarma has said in his book *The Poetry of Śankaradeva* published by the Forum for Śankaradeva Studies, Guwahati in 2000, 'In depth of feeling and structural ordinance, these poems bear comparison to the soul-stirring spiritual lyrics of Rabindranath Tagore (1861-1941) enshrined in the *Gitanjali*.' I wouldn't say that this was an uncommon feeling. In fact when Tagore's *One Hundred Poems of Kabir* was published in 1914, his English admirers were struck by the affinity with him. But perhaps these feelings are not enough to justify Tagore's place beside *bhakti* poets, Sants and Mahapurushas into the bargain. As I have said elsewhere, Sant Tagore would indeed be a travesty.

Besides, we are all aware of Tagore's versatility, a Goethe in the Indian dress, his 'Puja' songs being only a fraction of his total output. We may be also aware of his place in the Bengali consciousness, of how it is difficult for Bengalis to be left untouched by him—maybe he bears a comparison with Sankaradeva here with regard to his presence in the Assamese mind. My reading of the 'Puja' songs as texts immanent and without reference to the rest of Tagore, I hope, has not led us astray. *Bhakti* as the frame of reference was one way of containing that immanence.

2015: Sixth Srimanta Sankaradeva Lecture at Tezpur University

Nature in Tagore's Poetry

Those who had visited Santiniketan in the last years of Tagore's life tell us that they would often catch sight of him seated in an east-looking balcony before dawn as if he was waiting for light to appear. He seemed to be a part of the earth and the sky, of the dark frame of trees around and the faraway fading stars, producing a harmony that no one would dare break. It may remind us of Gorky's reminiscence of Tolstoy on the Black Sea beach, seated among the rocks like a rock himself, looking out to the waves, one who might get up any moment and order them into silence—a godlike presence whom Gorky dared not disturb. This was not Schiller's *sentimentalische* man[1] thirsting for Nature, not being a part of it. On the contrary this looked like Schiller's *naive* man, at one with Nature like the bird in the air or fish in the water. Interestingly, while speaking of Goethe, self-admittedly *naïve* as opposed to Schiller's own *sentimentalische*, Thomas Mann also thought of Tolstoy.[2] If he had known Tagore well enough

1 Friedrich Schiller, *Über naïve und sentimentalische Dichtung* (On Naïve and Sentimental Poetry), 1795.

2 'Goethe and Tolstoy,' in *Essays of Three Decades*, trans. H. T. Lowe-Porter (London: Secker and Warburg, 1947).

he might have thought of Tagore as well. The following words written by one of Tagore's successors in Bengali poetry a few months before Tagore's death are not only touching but telling:

> On the day we departed we saw the Poet in sick-bed. Little did I imagine what I would have to see. It was itself a shock to step into his room after the brilliant afternoon light spread all over sky and land. For the room was dark as night, lit only by a table-lamp burning in a corner. The Poet was reclining in what seemed to be an easy-chair, propped up by several pillows. He was quite still and his eyes were closed. A young doctor and one of his secretaries were attending. As we entered, he half opened his eyes and faintly uttered a few words. His right hand began to rise in blessing over our heads but dropped half way. I have not the words to say how I felt at the moment. It was as if the heart had received a sudden blow, I felt choked and overcome by a stupor so that I could not even have a full gaze at him. We could breathe freely only when we came out in the open. The immortal poet was a constant companion of this golden blaze of light while the frail earthen vessel lay imprisoned in a closed room.[3]

The spirit of the last words seems to agree with Prasanta Chandra Mahalanobis' idea of preserving Tagore's memory at Santiniketan. He was talking to Tagore's son Rathindranath a

---

3 Buddhadeva Bose, 'The Last Days of Tagore', in *Buddhadeva Basur Prabandhasamagra,* Vol. 3, *ed. cit.*, p. 500.

year after Tagore's death. Rather than a specific memorial, even a room with one of his paintings and a book by turn, it would be better to have a little space anywhere in Santiniketan's open, dressed with a hedge of flowers, for one to come and sit or stand.[4]

Indeed his Santiniketan was, among other things, Tagore's tryst to Nature, for not only was it 'a poet's school'[5] but also a latter-day *tapovana*. It cherished its environment, marked the seasons and held festivities to welcome them. As said in an article above, it also observed such annual events as the *Halakarshan*, the first laying of the plough and *Briksharopan*, the planting of saplings. Whatever words attended these festivities or events came from Tagore's pen, often in the form of *Gesamkunstwerke*. The total volume of such compositions is copious, much beyond what features as *Santiniketan* comprising his words mostly spoken at the weekly prayer. Apropos his *tapovana*, it may not be out of place to recall his reflections on the classic *tapovana* in Kālidāsa's *Śākuntala* where he highlighted its violation by the royal hunt as well as its contrast with the royal court—reflections put in perspective by comparison with Shakespeare's play of an apparently similar *donnée*, *The Tempest*. '*The Tempest*,' he said, 'is about oppression, punishment, discipline: *Śakuntalā* is about affection, peace, fellow feeling. Even taking the human form in *The Tempest* Nature has not been bound to

4 See Prasanta Chandra Mahalanobis' long letter after his first visit to Santiniketan after Tagore's death quoted in *Rabindranath / Prasantachandra Mahalanobis*, presented and ed. Uma Dasgupta (Kolkata: Ananda Publishers Private Ltd., 2002), pp. 18-25, especially the last two paragraphs.

5 See Rabindranath Tagore, 'A Poet's School,' in *Boundless Sky* (Calcutta: Visva-Bharati, 1964), pp. 231-250.

man by heartstrings; but while keeping their own shape in *Śakuntalā* the flora and fauna have been united with man in tender relationships.'[6]

This may take us back to an epiphany he had quite early in his career. He had begun rather self-ridden and prone to evening sadness. Then one morning as he was standing on the balcony of a Kolkata house and watching the sun rise from behind the neighbourhood trees, the world suddenly unfolded and light flooded his soul: 'I saw that the whole world was spread over with an uncommon glory, spreading everywhere in waves of joy and beauty.'[7] He called it 'awakening' or rather, the 'awakening of the pent-up spring from dreams'. Poems gushed forth like a waterfall, their thrust being 'I wonder how my heart is bared today, / and the world has come to embrace it.'[8] The epiphany is not only a landmark in Tagore's career but has long been turned into a symbol, and one should not be surprised to come across a book of poems some eight decades later bearing the title *Sudder Streeter Baranda* (Sudder Street's Balcony).[9]

Tagore's encounter with Nature came in a big way when he was looking after the family estates in Eastern Bengal and, as said above in a second article, was often moving in a houseboat on River Padma and its tributaries. The experience

---

6 'Śakuntalā,' *Prachin Sahitya* (Ancient Literature) in *Rabindra-Rachanabali* (Tagore's Collected Works), Vol. 10 (Kolkata: West Bengal Government, 1989), p. 124. Hereafter *RR*.

7 *Jibansmriti* (*My Reminiscences*), in *RR*, Vol. 11 (Kolkata: West Bengal Government, 1989), p. 73.

8 Ibid. p. 74.

9 Pranabendu Dasgupta, *Sudder Streeter Baaraandaa* (Kolkata: Krittibas Prakashani, 1966)

was recorded in a kind of *journaux intimes* though their leaves were meant to be letters to his niece Indira. Random pages from these leaves cum letters will reveal his sensations. Yet to take them as a mere transcript of *Bildung* or *Lehrjahre* would be limiting them, for while giving a hint here and there of his developing career, they confirm above all a sense of wonder in the infinite variety of natural phenomena. 'Living on in Kolkata,' he once wrote (November 1888), 'one forgets how actually beautiful this earth is. The sun setting everyday by this small river in the midst of peaceful trees, and thousands of stars coming up silently every night over this unbounded, grey, solitary, bare isle—how great an event all this is in the course of life is realised only if one lives here.' There is description of seasons, of gathering storms, of mornings and nights and noontide, of wide waters and tiny streams, of the everyday rhythm of rural life by the river—the endlessness of it all. 'This light, this air, this silence have gone into the roots of my hair and mixed with my bloodstream—this is my new daily intoxication, it is hard for me to describe it all'—so he wrote on 7 September 1894, and said further:

> Every autumn afternoon comes the same way to me—everyday the old renews as the new, and the very mood I had yesterday again revives. Nature doesn't in the least desist from daily repetitions. It is we who do that, for we feel that our language is not limitless and spacious enough to show forth the same old feeling as the new.

And on 2 July 1895:

> On turning my eyes to any side from where I am working, I see the blue sky mixed with the green earth at my doorstep—as if like a curious village girl Lady Nature is peeping through my window and door, and is adding beauty to my room and my mind, to my work and leisure.

One of his more familiar poems, 'Sonar Tari' ('The Golden Boat') seems to be embedded in this Nature, as the opening lines show:

> Clouds rumbling in the sky; teeming rain.
> I sit on the river-bank, sad and alone,
> The sheaves lie gathered, harvest has ended,
> The river is swollen and fierce in its flow.
> As we cut the paddy it started to rain.[10]

This feeling for Nature was in a way epitomised in the following entry to which attention has been drawn by Subha Chakraborty Dasgupta:

> I can somewhat recall the time when I was one with the earth, when the green grass grew upon me, the light of autumn fell on me, and in the rays of the sun the fragrant heat of youth rose from each pore of my green far-stretched limbs—when I lay sill spreading out on far and distant stretches of unknown lands, waters and mountains under the bright sky, the stream of joy and

---

10 Trans. William Radice, in *Rabindranath Tagore*: *Selected Poems* (Harmondsworth: Penguin Books, 1985), p. 53.

> a life-force would, in a very mute, semiconscious as well as in an immense manner, rise in me.[11]

Victoria Ocampo has told us that during Tagore's stay as her guest at San Isidro in Argentina in 1924 she tried to introduce him to Baudelaire. But the experience was not happy. When she was reading 'L'Invitation au voyage' to him with an oral English rendering, he told her halfway that he did not like her 'furniture poet'.[12] Was the reaction only to '*Des meubles luisants, / Polis par les ans, / Décoreraient notre chambre* …', or to the poem's thrust as such highlighting '*Là, tout n'est qu'ordre et beauté, / Luxe, calme et volupté*'? Abu Sayeed Ayyub who has written on Tagore as opposed to modernism would probably put the dislike more to the theme than language. Buddhadeva Bose who has translated Baudelaire into Bengali would put it to Tagore's unfamiliarity with contemporary reality.[13] Couldn't we also put it to a difference in their imagery, Baudelaire's urban, often antipathetic to Nature and Tagore's mainly rural,

11 *Chinnapatra*, in *RR*, Vol. 11, *ed. cit*., p. 337: trans. Subha Chakraborty Dasgupta, quoted in idem., 'Towards an Understanding of the *Baromasi*: Aspects of Lyric Poetry in Bengal,' in Earl Miner and Amiya Dev, eds. *The Renewal of* Song: *Renovation in Lyric Conception and Practice* (Calcutta: Seagull Books, 2002), p. 101.

12 Victoria Ocampo, 'Tagore on the Banks of the River Plate,' in *A Centenary Volume*: *Rabindranath Tagore 1861-1961* (New Delhi: Sahitya Akademi, 1961), p. 44. The issue of the 'furniture poet' came back in a homely humorous way in a letter Tagore later wrote to Ocampo apropos an arm-chair she had given him: 'I pass most of the day and a great part of the night deeply buried in your arm-chair which, at last, has explained to me the lyrical meaning of the poem of Baudelaire that I read with you.' Ibid. p. 45.

13 See *Kavi Rabindranath* (Tagore the Poet) (1966, rpt. Kolkata: Dey's Publishing, 1980), pp. 21-22n.

largely drawn on Nature? In a somewhat comparable poem called 'Sab-peyechi'r Desh' (The Land of Heart's Desire), in *Kheya*, the 'poetic' images are all discarded and replaced with images from Nature. It is a land where no one has a *mansion*, no *guards*, no *horses* in stables or *elephants* in chains, a land where no one lights a *crystal lamp* with *perfumed oil*, where no ladies dress their hair with *pearls*, and where temples have no *golden* spires—in other words, no *volupté*. Instead, it is a land where grass grows under the shadows of trees with a clear stream gurgling by, where creepers hang on wicker fences around huts with bees humming since morning, where people happily walk out at dawn to some work or other and come home at dusk with no wages. More such images, then again negation of the 'poetic' ones: no *traders* passing by in their boats stop here for business, no *armies* thump about with the roads shaken, no *royal chariot* appears, no faraway *traveller* seizes this land's charms overnight. There are no crowds here on the road, no ruckus in shops. Listen, poet, this is the land where to raise your hut. Wash the dust off your feet and put down your bundle. Tune up your strings, no need for further search. Stretch your legs here at day's end—under the starry sky; this is your land of heart's desire.

A catalogue of Tagore's images will reveal the pervasiveness of his Natural sources. He has the keenest sensation for all six seasons of the Bengali calendar: *grishma*, *varsha*, *sarat*, *hemanta*, *sit*, *vasanta*; and along with them of all the twelve months: *baisakh*, *jaishtha*, *ashadh*, *sraban*, *bhadra*, *asvin*, *kartik*, *agrahayan*, *paush*, *magh*, *phalgun*, *chaitra*. We shall come back to his love of seasons when we discuss his songs where a whole section is marked *Prakriti* (Nature).

No less is perhaps the sensation of *akas*, the sky which is a physical presence taking on a whole variety of hues ranging from the clearest blue to the deepest grey and giving reins to clouds, often white and often again dark, indeed the darkest at a certain time of the year. An image that might immediately come to mind is that of white rafts afloat on the azure; and another: clouds piling on clouds, darkness descending. There is an obvious link between the season and the colour of the sky and, where clouds show up, their colour. Of course his *akas* is also speckless, no less perhaps than Mallarmé's 'l'azur' ('De l'eternel azur la serene ironie'). Now *akas* being the home of wind, one has images of the mildest motion to wild turbulence. For instance the Bengal nor'wester can agitate a poem with heaps of clouds rolling and rushing in in a blind fury and defying resistance. The rest follows, producing a whole host of images involving grey, pallid fields, cattle on the run and the farmer chasing, boats splattering to the shore and the sail being fast pulled down, the split cloud in the western sky turning fiery and showing bloody eyes, and anxious birds flying away flock by flock across the lightning-rent emptiness. So builds up 'Barshasesh' (End of Year), referred to in an article above, a paean to Nature whose turbulence ends on a memorable calm.

The river is ubiquitous in Tagore, and so is the boat, whether to sail up or down, or to cross. That a whole batch of poems be called *Kheya* (Crossing) is not unexpected. The boat that sails up and at the lonely farmer's plea takes away his piled-up paddy but denies *him* room, is 'golden' because of the harvest's ripeness. Another boat performs an aimless voyage with a mysterious woman at the helm, scuttling across a westward sea, now turquoise now turbulent, with rich overtomes of vibrant hope and golden dreams, of doubt and uncertainty, of a *Weltschmerz* the German Romantics might have been envious of, and eventually of an easeful death. By treating it as an inevitable intertext and superimposing it on Rimbaud's 'Le Bateau ivre', a successor in Bengali poetry has proved this golden boat's world-worthiness of the order that Tagore himself had spoken of in a lecture he gave on 'World Literature' ('Visvasahitya'). I am speaking of Sudhindranath Datta's 'Jajati', a landmark in latter-day verse.

In terms of ubiquity, no less perhaps is the *way* that often brings in the image of a wayfarer along. 'Someone is there on the way, going, by giving out a call: how can I stay in'[14]—may instantly come to our mind with the hint of an incipient drama of waiting, whether or not we recognize it to be a reverse *abhisar* of the *Vaishnava Padavali* fame. A more telling instance of this composite image is found in the following poem:

> In deep shadows of rainy *Sraban*
> with secret steps,
> O, silent as night, you have come
> skirting all watch.
>
> Morning has shut its eyelids,
> wind in vain is howling,
> blue and bare sky is covered
> by a thick spread of cloud.
>
> Woodlands are hushed, no chirping,
> doors shut at every house,

14 See *Gitali*, 21.

> lone wayfarer, you alone
> are on wayfarer-free road.
>
> O, my lonely friend, my dearest,
> my door is left open,
> do not pass by like a dream
> pushing me in disdain. (*Gitanjali* 18: translation based on Tagore's own)

It would not be easy to list out the Nature-drawn images in Tagore. There are more areas, of trees and flowers and woods, of meadows and fields where cattle graze and the herd-boy plays the pipe, of steps going down to the river or pond, of village marts, and of many other things that had attracted his attention during the stay at the family estates and, as said above, been recorded in *Chhinnapatra*. Some had also gone into the stories he had written at the time. One such instance is:

> When he got into the boat and the boat took off, and the rain-swollen river was wet as it were with the overflowing tears of this earth, he felt a fierce pain in the heart—an insignificant village girl's sad face seemed to be expressing a huge world-wide sorrow. For a moment he wished, 'let me go back and bring along that destitute girl bereft of all worldly shelter'—but the sail by then had swollen, the rain-fed streams were flowing sharply, the village boundaries were disappearing and the cremation ground showed up—and the idea crossed the despondent heart of this traveller afloat the river, life is full of many such

separations, deaths, what is the good of going back!
Who is whose in this world anyway! ('Postmaster')

Tagore was too great a poet to have a summary view on Nature. Besides he was ever developing and writing newer and newer modes. If to celebrate Nature is to deny Culture, then we shall have to rethink his position. Here is a poem, *Balaka* (Wild Geese) 28 written in 1915, interestingly on the bank of Padma, his seat of *Chinnapatra*. A free translation would be:

The bird you have given song, it sings that song,
it doesn't give more.
Me you have given voice, I give more,
I sing.

The wind you have made free,
it serves you untrammelled.
Me you have given loads,
I go about with them, now bent, now up.
Losing them in death one by one
I bring them to your feet
free and unhampered to serve you;
bonds you gave me I turn to freedom.

To full moon you gave smiles;
happy dreams and pleasures
it pours, by filling earth's palms with nectar.
Sorrow you placed on my feverish forehead,

by soaking it over and over with tears
I turn it into joy and put it back to your hand
at day's end, in our night of union.

You have only made this clay earth
mixing darkness with light.
Putting me there empty-handed you
smile hiding behind that emptiness.
And give me the task
of building your paradise.

Others you only give,
from me alone you take.
What I offer in love,
stepping down from throne smiling
you clasp it to your heart.
You get back
more than you gave.

One may read a Nature-Culture antithesis in it, but one may also read some room for Culture in a world where Nature abounds. The moot question that seems to arise from this string of assertions is, could the Creator do without Man? In other words, couldn't Nature be enough? True Nature is mindless, but does this mindlessness produce, let us say, a Baudelairean response in Tagore? On the contrary, he recognises Nature's self-sufficiency and independence of Man. What seems to be mindlessness is perhaps a lack of drama, an eternity without ripples. One may be reminded here of Goethe's 'Prolog in Himmel' from *Faust* where the Archangels, after reporting severally to the Lord on the eternal state of Creation, say in unison:

> Der Anblick gibt den Engeln Stärke,
> Da keiner dich ergründen mag
> Und alle deine hohen Werke
> *Sind herrlich wie am ersten Tag.* (emphasis added)
>
> (The sight, as none can comprehend it,
> Gives strength to angels; thy array
> Of works, unfathomably splendid,
> *Is glorious as on the first day*. [trans. Walter Kaufmann])

It is then that Mephistopheles steps forward to report on Man. In other words, a clear distinction is made between Nature and Man. Of course Goethe is dealing with a different matter, Man's need of evil as a goad to srriving which alone redeems him. Indeed redemption is a principal Judaeo-Christian concern, and in spite of Goethe's post-Enlightenment orientation concomitant to the bourgeois value of Culture, he does have a redemptive frame. True his 'Ewig-Weibliche' ('Eternal-Feminine') is more a recall of tradition than Gretchen actually turning into a Beatrice; still the frame holds and we do not begin the poem with its celebrated nocturne, nor end it with no less celebrated 'Verweile doch, du bist so schön' ('Abide, you are so fair').

Unlike Goethe's, Tagore' Man is not hungering for happiness and hence rushing, at whatever costs, from one realm of Culture to another. His Culture consists in realising his place beside Nature, in not being envious of Nature's fullness and ashamed of his lack of it, but in giving what he can, his heart and mind and thus complement Nature. This is not to say that Man in Tagore has no sorrows or sufferings, and is never urged to move forward. History does give him occasions to surge and prove his worth. A moving poem by the name of 'Duhsamay' (1897: 'Hard Times') may come to our mind. Here are its first and last stanza in Buddhadeva Bose's adaptation:

> Music is silenced, the dark descending slowly
> Has stripped unending skies of all companions.
> Weariness grips your limbs and within the locked horizons
> Dumbly ring the bells of hugely gathering fears.
> Still, O bird, O sightless bird,
> Not yet, not yet the time to furl your wings.
>
> All that is past: your fears and loves and hopes;
> All that is lost: your words and lamentation;
> No longer yours a home nor a bed composed of flowers.
> For wings are all you have, and the sky's broadening courtyard,
> And the dawn steeped in darkness, lacking all direction.
> Dear bird, my sightless nird,
> Not yet, not yet the time to furl your wings![15]

The intent of these lines came to be clearer in a number of later poems. For instance, *Balaka* 37, a polysemic voyage poem, ends on: 'In the terrible night of suffering / by death hit / when man transcends his mortal bounds / will immortal divine glory not appear then?' And of course there is his Christ poem written on seeing the Passion Play at Oberammergau in

15 *Kavita*, Vol. 24, No. 2 (100, International Number, 1960), pp. 1-2.

1930, composed in English first as 'The Child' (subsequently rendered into Bengali). Its concluding lines are celebratory:

> The mother is seated on a straw bed with the babe on
> her lap,
> Like the dawn with the morning star.
> The sun's ray that was waiting at the door outside
> falls on the head of the child.
> The poet strikes his lute and sings out:
> 'Victory to Man, the new-born, the ever-living!'
> They kneel down,--the king and the beggar, the saint
> and the sinner,
> the wise and the fool,--and cry:
> 'Victory to Man, the new-born, the ever-living.'
> The old man from the East murmurs to himself:
> 'I have seen!'

Tagore was as much a poet of Man as of Nature, but without proposing a dichotomy between them. The dialectic of *das Leben* and *der Geist* of Thomas Mann would not have appealed to him. One reason perhaps of his antipathy to 'modernism' was in such dialectic. He was more at home with the Romantics. That the Romantics were not mere wide-eyed admirers of Nature but environmentalists has been long established. E. P. Thompson's study of Wordsworth set against the ravages of Nature by industrial capital in England was symptomatic of this rethinking.[16] Tagore's *Raktakarabi* (1926: Red Oleanders) is no less seminal in its critique of the mutilation of Nature.

16 See E. P. Thompson (posthumous), *The Romantics*: *England in a* Revolutionary *Age*, ed. Dorothy Thompson (New York: The New Press, 1997).

It focuses on industry's inroads into agriculture and on how industrial wage labour proves utterly uncreative and induces everyday dehumanisation, while industry's plain clothes police get more and more repressive. The ghost town or the *Yakshapuri* from which the play took its initial title, is surrounded by fields that are throughout the play reverberating with a harvest quire. And it is from these fields that the girl Nandini had come, giving the play its second subsequent title and motivating the uprising on which the curtain falls and which in all probability would end tragically.

As a precursor to all this we can think of a poem called 'Badhu' ('Bride'), written as early as 1888 and built around the sense of suffocation a young bride feels in the city having grown up in a village:

> 'Day's ending, let's go and fetch water.'
> I seem to hear from afar that old evening call—
> But where is the shade and the water?
> Where are the steps and the fig-tree?
> As I sit alone with my thoughts I seem to hear
> 'Day's ending, let's go and fetch water.'…
>
> Oh this city with its stony body!
> Its massive loveless fist has squeezed and crushed
> A young girl's feelings, pitilessly.
> Where are the boundless fields, the open path,
> The birdsong, the trees, the shadows?…
>
> I loiter here amidst them all,
> Each day hangs so heavily.

People here are like worms, crawling between bricks,
There is no love, there is no gaiety....

Master of sensation that he was, Tagore pushed it to a death wish:

They won't give love, they won't give light.
I feel all the time it would be good to die,
To sink in the lap of the water of the pool,
In its shady darkness, its cool black depths.[17]

Nature not only appears in Tagore as such, or as a background to Man and his Culture, but also as a portal to God. Poem after poem in *Kheya*, *Gitanjali*, *Gitimalya* and *Gitali* bear this out. Here are some instances in free translation:

Knowing I shall go out
someone seems to be waiting all day
by the blue sky.
Whispers pass from leaf to leaf,
on dark waves' crests
rock light's flickers—
knowing I shall go out. (from 'Ghater Path,' *Kheya*)

How
only one night's rain
has overflown

17 Trans. William Radice, in *Rabindranath Tagore*: *Selected Poems*, *ed. cit.*, pp. 47-49.

the pool in my room!
With eyes opened I saw
the dark blue water flooding around,
where are its shores, where bottom,
O tell me, tell—
look, the pool is filled up
in one rainfall. (from 'Prabhate,' *Kheya*)

A mild breeze has put
the pure white sail to flutter.
I have never seen
such steering.
From which seas it brings
what faraway riches!
My heart would float along,
leaving behind on this shore
all desires and gains.

Rains pour at the back
thunder rumbles,
sunrays fall on my face
from behind a splattered cloud.
Who are you, O steersman,
gem of whose joy and sorrow!
My mind wonders
to which tune to set the strings today,
to sing what song. (*Gitanjali*, 12)

If you gave me no love
then why filled up the morning sky

with such songs!
Why are stars strewn together,
and flowers form a bed,
why breathes the south breeze
a secret to my ears!

If you gave me no love
then why has the sky
such a loving look at me!
Then why from time to time
my crazy heart
puts the boat out on that sea
whose shores are not known to it! (from *Gitimalya*, 42)

In skies bloomed
the light's lotus.
Fold on fold the petals
spread on all sides,
the thick and deep waters of darkness
are all covered.
On the golden pistil at centre
seated am I in joy,
slowly around me
radiates the light's lotus. (from *Gitanjali*, 48)

You are back again as *Sraban*,
wearing a cloud wrap.
The sun is hidden, hidden are the stars,
the way is lost in dark,
in river rise waves.

All skies, all earth
are filled with words of rain.
Driven by a ceaseless patter
my dark night rings out,
it rings through my veins. (*Gitali*, 13)

Obviously there is no easy equation here between Nature and God. In other words Tagore is not a pantheist. Nature is often his setting for a tryst to God, or better, through Nature he has often an epiphany of God.

A good part of this Nature is seasonal. In *Gitabitan*, Tagore's Book of Songs there are 283 pieces devoted to *Prakriti*, their break-up being: 9 introductory + 16 + 115 + 30 + 5 + 12 + 96, devoted respectively to summer, rains, early autumn, late autumn, winter and spring. Writing seasons, we know, is an old poetic practice. Vālmīki's description of *varsha* in the 'Kishkindhākāṇda' with Rāma waiting for the right season to attack Laṅkā with Sugrīva's help, is a classic by all standards and has influenced much later poetry, above all Kālidāsa. And apropos Kālidāsa's *Meghadūta*, we are reminded of a longish poem Tagore wrote in a rainy afternoon of 1890, called 'Meghaduta'. Here are some excerpts:

Ah, supreme poet, that first, hallowed day
Of Ashadh on which, in some unknown year, you wrote
Your *Meghadūta*! Your stanzas are themselves
Like dark-layered sonorous clouds, heaping the misery

Of all separated lovers throughout the world
Into thunderous music.

Who can say what thickness of cloud that day,
What festiveness of lightning, what wildness of wind
Shook with their roar the turrets of Ujjayini? …

All this time, companionless people have sat in loveless rooms
Through the long, rain-weary, starless evenings of Ashadh.
In faint lamplight, they have slowly read aloud that verse
And drowned into their loneliness.
Their voices come to me from your poem;
They sound in my ear like waves on the sea-shore. …

Today is a dark day; the rain is incessant,
The wind ferocious—treetops rise
Like arms at its attack; their swishing is a cry.
Lightning dart through the clouds, ripping them,
Dotting the sky with sharp, crooked smiles.

In a gloomy closed room I sit alone
And read the *Meghadūta*. My mind leaves the room,
Travels on a free-moving cloud, flies far and wide. …

The vision goes. I watch the rain again
Pouring steadily all around.
The darkness thickens, the solitariness of night approaches.
Far across the plain, the wind moans aimlessly.[18]

18 Trans. William Radice, 'The *Meghadūta*', in *Rabindranath Tagore*: *Selected Poems*, *ed. cit*., pp. 50-52.

Kālidāsa also wrote *Ṛtusaṁhāra*, a poem of all seasons, a calendar as it were of lovers' moods, but it is hard to say if Tagore had as much to do with that as with *Meghadūta*. Influence hunters may see if James Thomson's *Seasons* had cast a long shadow on Tagore by way of the English Romantic poets, especially Keats, or through his predecessor Biharilal Chakravarti whose love of Nature left a telling impact on him. They may even try to locate if he had heard Vivaldi's *Four Seasons* on one of his early trips overseas. However, what needs to be remembered is that his appreciation of seasons had also an environmental as well as a festive import, as clearly shown by individual season plays and a comprehensive *mis-en-scène* composed in 1926, *Nataraj Riturangasala* (Siva's Dance of Seasons).

Tagore's perception of the seasons as expressed in *Prakriti* is naturally not embedded in words alone but also in the melody. Of course his lyrics are incomparable, the best in the language, and may be read as perfect poems. So, even though they are often stored in our memory as words cum melody, I am quoting his seasonal songs' specimens here in words—and that too in my inept English rendering.

Grishma (Summer)

> Heart pierced in thirst by fierce fires.
> Night sleepless, and day long and burning,
> no respite, none.
> On dried orchard-branch the tired dove
> coons a sad plaintive note.
> Yet there is no fear, we keep looking up at sky.
> For you know you will appear one day
> like turbulence to our parched-up souls.

Varsha (Rains)

Rain pours in torrents today this full season,
sky-split streams keep falling uncontained.
In Sal forests from time to time rocks a thunder storm,
waters flow this way and that way over the fields.
Brandishing the cloud's locks who is it dancing this day?
Look, my mind is rain-struck, is won over by storm—
at whose feet falls this wave overflowing my heart!
What tumult is inside today, all doors are unbolted—
the madman in heart wakes up this month of Bhadra.
Who has gone so wild today both outside and inside!

Sarat (Early Autumn)

What guest has come to our life-doors in Sarat?
Sing out jubilation, O heart, sing out jubilation.
Let the blue sky's silent words and dew-soaked eagerness
ring out in your *veena*'s strings today.
Join in with same verve the golden song of paddy fields,
set adrift the tunes in the clear streams of the full river.
Look with deep content at the face of the one who has come,
throw open the door and go out with him.

Hemanta (Late Autumn)

In dewy nights those lamps of sky
have been hidden by autumn behind her shawl.
She called out to all homes, 'hang lamps this diwali,
hang your own lamps, and dress up the earth with lights.'
Empty is your flower garden now, magpie and cuckoo
aren't singing.
grassy *kash* withers away on river bank.

Let fatigue and sadness go, light lamps in diwali—
your own lamps light, let lights' celebration ring out.
Gods today are waiting—wake up, earth's boys and girls.
waken the night with lights.
Dark descends, and day ends, light lamps in diwali,
your own lamps light, and conquer this night.

Sit (Winter)

Winter winds began dancing in *amlaki*-branches.
The leaves shiver and keep falling rhythmically.
A whirl came and snatched all away.
No fruits could hope to have any future hues.
Whose play it is to empty and fill up then
for him now we wait all day.
Look, winter's touch from time to time is felt around,
when will my final hour come to lose all, at what dawn?

Vasanta (Spring)

Spring is alive at your door,
don't turn it away
from your hooded shame-ridden life.
Unfold your heart-petals,
forget who is yours and who is not,
in this song-filled sky
raise waves of your fragrance.
Losing track in world outside
shower loads of sweetness abroad.
In woods a deep sadness rings
through the branches today,
waiting for someone in a distant sky

the eager earth is dressed up.
South breeze blows over my heart,
pounding from door to door for someone—
this fragrance-drunk night
is awake at someone's feet on earth.
O beautiful, O beloved, darling,
whom do you call in your deep tones!

Tagore has a book of poems on trees called *Banabani* (1926: Message of the Forest). He said in its introduction:

> The call of those dumb friends of mine who, carried away by their love of light have stretched their hands to the sky, reached my soul. Their language is the earliest language of the world of life …
>
> These trees are the single string of the world-*baul*—they have thrills of simple tunes in their marrow, dance of the one-beat rhythm in their branches and leaves. If we hear in silence with all heart then a message of liberation reaches our soul. This liberation lies on the shores of that immense sea of life at whose upper streams is the play of the beautiful in waves of infinite hues, and deep down, '*śāntam śivam advaitam*'. There is no greedy desire in that play, no hypnosis, no inertia, only the waves of interminable joy issuing from the absolute.…
>
> A vaishnava woman once asked, when shall we have union under the tree? That means, if we can

> full-heartedly breathe in the pure tune of life flowing through the tree then the union-song will not be jarring. In Buddhadeva's gospel we also seem to hear the gospel of the Bodhi-tree under which he attained enlightenment—the two gospels are fused. The forest seers could hear the gospel of the tree, '*vṛkṣa iva stavdho divi tiṣṭhyekaḥ*'. They heard, '*yadidaṁ kiṁca sarvaṁ prāṇa ejati niḥsṛtam*'. In trees they heard that interrogation of all time, '*kena prāṇaḥ prathamaḥ praitiyuktaḥ*'—wherefrom has first life come to this universe with its dynamism? That *praiti*, that dynamism would never stop, and ever gushed forth the stream of forms—how infinite their lines, their gestures, their idiom, their sensations! Where else does one have the great liberation of feeling deeply within oneself, with all purity, the ever newer and newer manifest flow of eternal creation by that first *prāṇapraiti* or life-dynamism?

The very first poem of *Banabani* is 'Brikshabandana' ('In Praise of Trees'), an encomium to the tree set to a high tone and giving a comprehensive idea of its primal nature and value. It begins as a regular ode:

> O Tree, life-founder, you heard the sun
> Summon you from the dark womb of earth
> At your life's first wakening; your height
> Raised from the rhythmless rock the first
> Hymn to the light; you brought feeling to harsh,
> Impassive desert.

It ends too with a similar apostrophe after an enumeration of the tree's greatness:

O sun-drinker,
The fire with which—by milking hundreds
Of centuries of days of sunlight—
You have filled your core, man has received
As your gift, making him world-mighty,
Greatly honoured, rival to the gods:
Man, whose life is in you, who is soothed
By your cool shade, strengthened by your power,
Adorned by your garland—O tree, friend
Of man, dazed by your leafy flutesong
I speak today for him as I make
This verse-homage, As I dedicate this offering
To you.[19]

Along with 'Brikshabandana' is a poem in *Banabani* called 'Jagadishchandra', a poem of dedication to his friend Jagadish Chandra Bose who had done pioneering work in plant physiology establishing their life-reactions or *élan vital*. Indeed nothing could be more fitting, as the poem in so many words shows:

Thus life had its first speech all around
in grasses, in woods, yet it was hidden away,
we did not hear it; O sage, you with single-minded devotion
gave language to the mute; heard the forest's
sentiments in your seclusion; the sorrows of mute life

19 Trans. William Radice, in *Rabindranath Tagore: Selected Poems*, *ed. cit.*, pp. 91-93.

> that ever raised a throbbing sensation in earth's breast
> by bursting into buds, spreading into hundred branches,
> giving a motion to leaves, and having tortuous roots
> rocked by life and death—this mystery was
> all revealed to you on a sudden.
> Life's eager words from mute insides
> you brought to light across darkness.

In fact a major theme of the *Banabani* poems is *mauna* or muteness that his friend unlocked and he in his phenomenal intuition as a poet deciphered. For instance, the poem about the creeper that he had named 'nilmani' or sapphire has a leitmotiv as it were in the word *mauna*:

> The load of muteness
> The sky cannot bear…
>
> Earth's deep muteness casts a blue shadow on the distant hill.
>
> The muteness that seeks itself in the blue of the sea,
> that endless muteness has overflowed the bunches of the
>   blue flower…

The flower is not only the symbol of muteness made speech but also an emblem of the *praiti* Tagore spoke of in the introduction. In its blue is Nature's dynamism manifest.

Tagore's dedication to Jagadish Chandra Bose is also proof that he looked at science in terms of Nature. No doubt science is method, but by being *meta hodos*, it presupposes phenomena or Nature. Unless Nature is there or unless Nature strikes us with wonder or a sense of mystery, there may not be any science. So, in spite of all its achievements that testify to human worth, Nature's primacy is not denied. There poetry is science's kin, for Nature is poetry's principal *donnée*. I have a mind here to call Baudelaire Tagore's antipodes—both are great. That Tagore had two other themes, Man and God, Man taking him to Time and God away from Time, is not in contradiction to his commitment to Nature. His Time-bound Man is not out to destroy Nature; his Timeless God does not leave out Nature. Between themselves his Man and God may have many uneasy moments—his God may not answer all his Man's doubts, his Man may not always have unquestioned faith in God—Tagore was no simple poet without twists and turns. But his Nature never falters and he never fails Nature. One of his last poems (*Arogya, 31*) is:

> Soon, I feel the time comes near to leave.
> With sunset shadings
> screen the parting day.
> Let the hour be silent; let it be peaceful.
> Let not any pompous memories or meetings
> create a sorrow's trance.
> May the trees at the gate
> raise the earth's chant of peace
> in a cluster of green leaves.
> May the night's blessings be
> in the light of the seven stars.[20]

2011: in Roddam Narasimha, ed. Nature and Culture, *PHISPC, XIV. 1 (New Delhi: Centre for Studies in Civilizations)*

20 Trans. Amiya Chakravarty, in *A Tagore Reader*, *ed. cit*., p. 375.

Tagore and Sikhism

When I was at school a poem I would often recite at a gathering was Tagore's 'Bandi Bir' (Prisoner Hero) celebrating Sikh heroism and martyrdom. Some of its lines I still remember, especially the ones at the beginning: '*pancanadir tire / beni paakaaiyaa sire / dekhite dekhite gurur mantre / jaagiyaa utheche sikh / nirmam nirbhik*' (By banks of five rivers / with hair tied in braids / in no time did Sikhs wake up / in Guru's name / unrelenting and fearless). Their wake-up slogans were 'Alakh Niranjan' and 'Victory to the Guru'. And

> A day came
> when millions knew no fear
> nor had debts to any.
> Life and death were mere footmen,
> and heart free of worries.
> By the ten banks of five rivers
> such a day did come.

With this awakening in the background, the poem goes on into the Mughal offensive out of envy and fear, and the heroic battle put up by the Sikhs until their fort at Gurudaspur falls with the leader Banda [Bahadur] taken prisoner. Carnage follows. In seven days seven hundred Sikhs are beheaded their spirit of martyrdom contesting for places of priority in the beheading. Then the worst comes. One of Banda's infant sons is thrown into his lap with the express order of killing him. This involves both father and son in martyrdom. The poem narrates how Banda quells his son's fear by whispering the magic spell of martyrdom to his ears, 'Victory to the Guru'. Yes, it is with 'Victory to the Guru' on his lips that the young martyr readies himself for his martyr father's dagger. The act of most dastardly infanticide is most lovingly done throwing waves of silence and shock through the executioners' court. Banda follows suit with hot pincers tearing his body apart. Across these sixty-five years I still remember the emotion in my voice in spelling out the last words of the poem: '*darsakjan mudilo nayan*, / *sabhaa holo nistabdha*' (The spectators shut their eyes, and the court / went dead silent).

The date these fourteen lyric stanzas comprising the narrative poem 'Bandi Bir' were composed, was November 1899. The poem was part of a book of poems called *Katha* (Tales: 1899) containing narrative poems on ancient and medieval Indian material. Its prefatory note was: 'The Buddhist tales narrated in this book are taken from Rajendralal Mitra's collection in English of Buddhist literature of Nepal. The Rajput stories have been found in Todd's Rajasthan and the Sikh narratives in one or two English Sikh histories. I have got the Vaishnava tales from Bhaktamal. Some difference from the original sources will be noted in these poems—I hope in accordance with common literary practice I shall not be held punishable for such change.' In other words, in a mild way Tagore is saying that his narratives are not versified history but depiction of experience derived from history. And the purpose is not edification but appreciation.

There are two other 'Sikh' poems in *Katha*, one on Bhai Toru Singh's martyrdom, 'Prarthanatita Daan' (Gift beyond Prayer), and the other 'Sesh Siksha' (Last Lesson) on Guru Gobind Singh's self-sought retribution cum death. This second I shall take up with the two other Guru Gobind Singh poems he had written earlier in 1888. 'Prarthanatita Daan' is short enough to be quoted whole:

Gift beyond Prayer (Prarthanatita Daan)

> For a Sikh cutting his braided hair is as bad as giving up religion.
>
> When the Pathans brought
> the Sikh prisoners in chains—
> Suhridganj's soil
> went blood-red.
> Nawab said, 'Listen, Torusingh,
> I wish to pardon you.'
> Torusingh said, 'why
> this dishonour to me?'
> Nawab replied, 'You are a great warrior,
> I am not angry with you,
> all I ask for is that you
> cut your braid for me.'
> Torusingh said, 'Your kindness
> is imprinted on my heart—

> I shall give you more than you have asked,
> my head with the braid.'

This came in close heels of 'Bandi Bir' (only a Rajput poem intervening) in November 1899. Its history is scanty, may even be inexact, yet it bears the essence of Sikh martyrdom. It concerns the first of the five K's of Khalsa Panth, *kesh* which being a gift of God is inseparable from the head. To cut it is to disown the head. Indeed Toru Singh's repartee hits the bull's eye. And surely the Nawab knew it. In apparent innocence he is asking a Sikh to give up his faith. Is he testing him, to see if he sells his faith in order to save his head? But isn't there a contradiction in terms here in the Khalsa perspective—how can you save your head by sacrificing what grows on it? (It may be an idle comparison with Hebrew Samson, yet it strikes one. Sikh religious historians may tell us better.) So martyrs are those that offer to die to defend the purity of their faith, to save it from any doubts or innuendos. The Nawab's 'request' conceals a call to heresy, or contrarily, without his knowing it, to martyrdom. Fallen among vengeful enemies a Sikh leader is by definition a martyr. The Nawab is only a factor.

There are in all three Guru Gobind Singh poems, two written earlier and the third within a few days of the Toru Singh poem. The earlier poems occur in Tagore's first major book of poems containing a whole variety of themes, *Manasi* (Lady of the Mind: 1890). Written on consecutive days, in 1888, they are built around Guru Gobind Singh's *sadhana*. The first one, named 'Guru Gobinda', is a long dialogue Guru Gobind Singh has with his disciples—he speaking and they listening. They have come to take him back to the land of the five rivers from his seclusion (' "Friends, go back, / it is not time yet"—/ night ending, on Jamuna's banks / of low hills, and a dense forest; / Guru Gobinda said aloud / to his six disciples.'). Laid out in twenty-five lyric stanzas, it is a narrative poem of the kind Tagore would later develop in *Katha*. Guru Gobind Singh is fully aware of the pull—the many tasks awaiting his leadership—in fact he has a full vision of them. The poet is doing justice to history but in his own way, through a set of dreams as it were. But Guru Gobind Singh wakes up, for his *sadhana* is not yet over.

> I must still be in the world of imagination,
> and have my seat in the forest—
> still I need only quiet contemplation,
> lonely meditation without action,
> night and day to listen sedentarily
> to my soul's voice. …
>
> Twelve years have thus passed,
> how longer do I have to go—
> by acquiring eternal life
> drop by drop from all sides
> when in myself shall I see
> my Self in all fullness?
>
> When I shall open my heart and say—
> 'I have attained my end.
> You all follow me,
> The Guru is calling you— …'

The second Guru Gobind Singh poem, 'Nishphal Upahar' (Fruitless Gift), is complementary to the first, depicting the Guru's composure in the midst of his *sadhana* not swayed by any nostalgic dreams of the future. His portrait is perfect: no eddies in his heart as in the river below where the scene is laid for the poem. It is Jamuna as in the first, and its banks are as hilly and full of shingles. A classical motif for such *sadhana* to be tested out is temptation, which often comes in the form of some greed-evoking possession, whether a nymph or riches. Tagore seemed so touched by its theme that he wrote the poem twice on the same day, with slight variations in the metre, the rhyme scheme remaining the same, *aabb*. Here are some lines from its twelve stanzas (I am quoting from the second version):

> When Raghunah arrived
> the Sikh Guru was reading a life of the Lord.
> Touching his feet Raghu said,
> 'master, the servant has brought you a small gift.' …
>
> Two golden bangles inlaid with gems
> Raghu placed at the Guru's feet with folded hands.
>
> Picking them up from the ground
> the master looked them over with moving fingers. …
>
> Smiling a little the Guru put them aside,
> and went back to the book he was reading.
> Suddenly one bangle from the rock it was on
> rolled down into Jamuna's stream.

Raghunath with shouts of 'alas oh alas'
jumped into the water with outstretched hands, …

Not once did the Guru raise his face,
so intense was his joy of reading. …

Daylight faded out with the day,
nothing was found scuttling up Jamuna.
In wet clothes, empty hands, tired with bent head
Raghunath came back to the Guru.

'I can still retrieve it,' he begged with folded hands,
'if you show me where it is lying.'
By flinging the second bangle into water
the Guru said, 'there it is on the riverbed.'

The third Guru Gobind Singh poem, 'Sesh Siksha' (Last Lesson), is a narrative of a different order. The Guru is at the end of his career and is not fully sure that his dreams have come true. The Bharat he had looked forward to is now 'narrow, split-up, doubt-ridden'. 'Has he been wrong then, / his life a failure?' The poem begins with a pensive Guru in the throes of despair. The turn of events that follows—the Pathan from whom he had bought a horse claiming payment, he deferring, the Pathan calling him names, he in a fit of rage beheading the Pathan—despairs him further: 'I can see / my time is up. My sinful sword / has belied its ideals / by shedding blood for nothing. In my arm / I have no more any faith. / I must wash up this sin and shame--/ from today let that be my life's last task.' Expiation begins. He raises the Pathan's son as his own, showers on him love and care, instructs him in both scriptures and arms—all to the amazement and apprehension of his followers. 'What is this, master, what are you doing? / We fear the consequence.' But his expiation has given him back his self-confidence: he has become the 'Bir (Heroic) Guru' again. He knows what he is doing, raising a worthy avenger of his father. As to the Pathan boy, he becomes a son to him, 'loves him / like life—is ever by his side, / as if he is his right hand.' All his own sons having died in battle, this boy fills up the vacuum in his heart. Tagore uses an image here. The Guru is like a thunder-struck banyan that has had a seed brought by wind from outside into its hollow, growing into a tree itself that covers the old banyan with its own branches.

Once the Pathan boy's instruction is over, he begs leave of his foster father to go out into the world to prove his worth. The Guru tells him that there is one more lesson left. It is the lesson that he has been all these years waiting to give his foster son, the retribution that he owes for his utterly mindless and bloody act committed years ago. The son must avenge his father. One evening he takes the boy with him leaving behind his followers, to the spot where he had killed the father. It is by a river. 'The fading day's burnt-out crimson light / casting a long shadow like a bat's wings / is flying to the western wilderness / in the silent sky.' The Guru tells the boy to dig in the sand. A reddened stone is found the red of which is identified as the boy's father's blood. 'The day is come … by killing your father's killer / in hot blood quench / his thirsty soul.' The boy has an instantaneous reaction, but the next moment he throws himself at the Guru's feet saying, 'Do not play / this devilish game. God knows / I have forgotten my father's murder; you /

I have known as father, guru and friend / all this time. Let that love fill up the mind, / and let rage wither under it.' Since then the Pathan boy avoids the Guru's intimate company, until at a chess game he is confronted with him. The boy keeps losing and the game lingers into the night. They are alone now and with his head bent the boy thinks up moves. Suddenly the Guru flings a chessman at him and roaring with laughter says, 'How can such a coward win / who plays with his father's killer?' Provoked into murderous rage the boy instantly unsheathes his dagger and plunges it into the Guru's breast, and the Guru says smilingly, 'At last you have learnt / to avenge injustice. / This was your last lesson—the last time today / I bless you, my son.'

The three Guru Gobind Singh poems are of three different tempers. The first shows him eager to finish his gestation and become the Guru he is to be. That future seems to be pulling him though he does not mean any compromise with his remaining *sadhana*. But it surely lacks the unruffledness of the second poem. There the *sadhana* is as it were in its essence while in the first it is put in perspective. The third is expiatory. And as in all expiations it is preceded by a fall and ends on a rise. But it is an expiation that his followers cannot quite comprehend. At the end of his life Guru Gobind Singh also proves to be an ideal individual. Perhaps in advance this answers some of the doubt Tagore is going to raise in an essay on him in 1910 in contradistinction with Shivaji and, especially, in the background of the Nanak Panth.

Tagore has a sixth 'Sikh' poem, but written much later, in 1935. A variation on 'Bandi Bir' it reiterates his admiration for Sikh heroism and martyrdom. And by being an utterance in the last decade of his life it has an abiding significance. But before getting to it let us recall his series of three historical essays written as early as 1885 for *Balak* (Boy), a magazine meant for the younger members of the Jorasanko household. They were 'Kajer Lok Ke' (Who is a Worthy Person?), 'Bir Guru' (Heroic Guru) and 'Sikh-Svadhinata' (Sikh Independence). They deal respectively with Guru Nanak, Guru Gobind Singh, and Banda Bahadur and after. His main source was J. D. Cunningham's *A History of the Sikhs* (1849). He might have also looked at W.L. M'Gregor's *The History of the Sikhs* (1846)—might have, for there is no evidence as such though he did hint at more than one English Sikh history in his preface to *Katha* from which we quoted three poems. The first essay is about the two worlds of Nanak's father and Nanak. Nanak's father was materially minded and wanted his son to have equal materiality. But Nanak had immaterial longings. Tagore quoted the *khara sauda* episode that proved their difference of values. The Sultanpur episode didn't mean a tilt, for though he worked at the granaries his mind was elsewhere. And then he had that epiphany in the Muslim fakir admonishing him upon which he left home. His *udasi* is taken up in some detail: '… Nanak travelled to many places and countries, doing as much good as he could to people and preaching the religious truth to all. He loved both Hindus and Muslims. But he pointed out whatever was wrong with Hinduism. He also pointed out whatever was wrong with Islam. Yet both Hindus and Muslims were devoted to him.' Back home he gave spiritual advice to everyone. 'He told them to worship one God, be religious, forgive others' sins, and love all.' Tagore ends his essay with a lesson for his juvenile readers: 'Now judge if it was Kalu [Bedi] or Kalu's son Nanak who was worthier. The Sikhs you see today whose handsome built, noble countenance, great strength and unlimited courage astonish you, this people are Nanak's sishya. There were no Sikhs before Nanak. Such a noble race has been born out of Nanak's noble thought and religiosity. The money made by Kalu had filled up his own belly, and the religious riches earned by Nanak have been feeding men for four hundred years. Who then was worthier?'

The very title of the second essay, 'Heroic Guru', implies its subject, Guru Gobind Singh. 'The nobleness with which Nanak was born did not extinguish with his death. The religious hymns he sang, the songs of joy and hope, went on reverberating. Newer and newer Gurus came up to lead the Sikhs to greatness.' Tagore raises the curtain on Mughal hostility to the Sikhs and tells his juvenile readers of the Ninth Guru Tegbahadur's sacrifice at Aurangzeb's court to keep the secrecy of the Sikh doctrine. His son Gobind, the Tenth Guru, pledged Sikh consolidation, but he went through a twenty-year intense *sadhana* for that (the subject of the first *Manasi* poem we quoted). He abolished caste among Sikhs and conferred a common surname, Singh, on the males. To illustrate his utter disregard for riches, Tagore tells the story of Guru Gobind's refusal to accept a pair of expensive bangles from a rich disciple (the subject of the second *Manasi* poem). His continuous struggles to establish Sikh supremacy and battles against Muslims are given in some detail. A correspondence with Aurangzeb is quoted in which he accused the Mughals of atrocities against the Sikhs and added: 'My sons have been killed; all my ties to the world are snapped; I am waiting for death; I don't fear anyone, I only fear the sole emperor of the world, the King of all kings. The prayer of the poor to God does not go unanswered; one day you shall have to account for all your oppression and cruelties.' Anyway his worth was finally recognised in the Mughal court. But Guru Gobind Singh died under strange circumstances, at the hands of a Pathan whose father he had impetuously killed, and whom he had raised as his son giving all training so that he could one day avenge his father's death on him. It is this that Tagore later develops into the poem 'Last Lesson'. Tagore's conclusion on the 'Heroic Guru' for his juvenile readers is: 'Though Guru Gobind did not succeed in fulfilling the resolution to which he had dedicated his life, yet it was chiefly he who turned the Sikhs into a martial people. After his death the Sikhs one day attained their independence; but it was he who had opened the door to that independence.'

Tagore's third essay picks up the thread from the second and deals with the eventual fulfilment of Guru Gobind Singh's pledge of 'freeing his people from the foreign oppressors'. The crucial role was played here by Guru Gobind's immediate successor, Banda [Bahadur]. Some of his exploits are quoted taking the region by storm. Finally the decisive battle of Gurudaspur is narrated around which gravitate those resonant stanzas of 'Bandi Bir'. The Sikhs lost and the Mughals won. But the history was like a seesaw, defeats were followed by victories. Again some defeats were as ghastly as that of Gurudaspur demanding martyrdom. The tale of Toru Singh comes in here, lying at Suhridganj (Suhidganj?), Lahore who had refused to cut his long hair (forbidden in Sikhism) and instead offered his head with it—subject of the short poem we quoted. Seesawing further, history rolls on. And Tagore ends the essay with—'After all that long the Sikhs were fully independent. Guru Gobind's purpose was partly attained. Then rose Ranjit Singh. Afterward roared the British lion. And after that gradually all India went red. Ranjit Singh's famous prophecy came true.'

These three instructive essays and five narrative poems presuppose an admiration for Sikhism which goes back to Tagore's visit to Amritsar at eleven in 1873. He had just had his sacred thread ceremony and was on his way to the Himalayas with his father, Maharshi Debendranath, at the latter's instance. They stopped at Amritsar for a month. His father had been to Amritsar before and stayed there for a couple of months, in fact before the poet's birth, and was immersed in the Nanak Panth like his contemporaries in the Bengal Brahmo circles. In *Jibansmriti* (1912: *My Reminiscences*) Tagore recalls the boy Rabindranath's sense of wonder at the Golden Temple:

> I remember the Gurudarbar at Amritsar like a dream. Many days with father I walked to that Sikh temple in the middle of a lake. Prayers were being said there all the time. My father would sit among those Sikh worshippers and would suddenly join in the prayer singing; on hearing these songs of devotion from an outsider they would be impressed and honour him. … Once he had a singer from the Gurudarbar come to our house and sing *bhajans* for him.

But Debendranath had gone through all this before, especially the joining in the Sikh prayer singing at the Gurudarbar, when he had been at Amritsar some years ago. In fact it was then that he had collected the famous *sabad* of Nanak's:

> gagan mai thaalu ravi-candu dipak bane
> tarikaamandal janak moti
> dhupu malaanlo pavanu cavaro kare
> sagal banaraai phulanta joti
> kaisi aarati hoi
> bhavakhandanaa teri aarati
> anahataa sabad baajanta bheri

He had it printed in the periodical *Dharmatattva* in 1872. Its Bengali translation, presumably by Debendranath himself, was repeatedly printed in *Tattvabodhini Patrika* in 1873 and 1875. Whoever had set that translation to music, whether Debendranath himself or his son Jyotirindranath, one of Rabindranath's elder brothers, it was Jyotirindranath who set the music to score. Rabindranath must have sung it in Brahmo festivals—it did appear in his book of songs. Anyway, the Bengali text is:

> gaganer thaale ravi chandra dipak jvale,
> taarakaamandal chamake moti re.
> dhup malayaanil, pavan chaamar kare,
> sakal banaraaji phulanta jyoti re.
> keman aarati, he bhavakhandana, tava aarati—
> anaahata sabda baajanta bheri re.

The *aarati* motif in this *bhajan* may remind us of a song Tagore was going to write in 1884, 'taanhaare aarati kare chandra tapan':

Him the moon and sun do *aarati*, to His feet bow gods and men,
seated is that refuge of universe in His worldly shrine.
Time without beginning and skies without end are filled with
    that boundless splendour
where waves rise from the depths what joy oh joy
while bearing the six seasons in hand the earth pours flowers
    at His feet,
of many colours, of much fragrance, of many tunes and rhythms.
The sky fills up with birds' singing—sing clouds sings ocean—
big winds go rushing in mirth, tune up in mountain caves.
How many hundreds of devotees are gazing joyously, and
    singing songs—
in holy light blooms love, and all illusions shatter.

(Vivekananda was said to have been fond of this song.) Some of Tagore's songs of the time, the so-called *brahmasamgit*, might not have been out of tune with Guru Nanak's songs. Let me quote two samples from the two successive years, 1885 and 1886:

How go on with this sojourn here!
Live through such doubt and heartache and mourning!
Who will save us in sorrow-fear-and-anxiety—
there is none so dear, alas, in this wilderness.
(1885)

Give light to the blind, give life to the dead—
you are kindness-nectar's ocean, give a drop of your kindness.
Dry is my heart like a hard stone,
water my dried-up eyes in love's shower.

Him who doesn't call out to you, you keep calling in.
Him who goes away from you, you keep pulling in.
The thirsty that goes about your ambrosia-ocean's shores
you soothe in sprays of affection, and feed ambrosia.
I had once found you, but then lost you in neglect,
I fell asleep, and see darkness around my eyes.
Whom do I tell my *viraha*, who will console me,
year passes after year, your loving face I don't see—
show me yourself, oh show me, my dying heart is crying out.
(1886)

The second song might have had a special power of sustenance to the poet, for some thirty-six years later he was once heard humming it all through a late night. The witness was young Prasanta Chandra Mahalanobis, a close associate (later famed as the founder director of Indian Statistical Institute) who had arrived late on a festive eve at Santiniketan and was given for lack of accommodation a cot in Tagore's room only a few feet from Tagore's own cot.

We recall that it was in 1885 that he wrote those three instructive 'Sikh' essays. The years 1888 and 1899 were again dates for his five 'Sikh' poems. The next dates were 1909, 1910 and 1914—the first for the translation of a Sikh *bhajan*, the second for a critique of Guru Gobind Singh, and the third for the translation of a second Sikh *bhajan*. The first Sikh *bhajan* is:

baadoi baadoi ramyabinaa baadoi.
amal kamal bic
ujal rajani bic
kaajar ghana bic

nisa aadhiyaaraa bic
bina ranan sunaaye.
baadoi baadoi ramyabinaa baadoi.

Tagore's Bengali version is:

baaje baaje ramyabinaa baaje—
amalkamalmaajhe, jyotsnaarajanimaajhe,
kaajalghana-maajhe, nisi-aandhaar-maajhe,
kusumsurabhi-maajhe binaaranan suni je
preme preme baaje.

He has departed a little by adding 'kusumsurabhi-maajhe' (in the fragrance of flowers) and changing the last line's 'ramyabinaa' into 'preme preme' (in love). However, in his Bengali song developed from this he has two more stanzas, one beginning 'naache naache ramyataale naache' (dances in a lovely beat) and the other, 'saaje saaje ramyabese saaje' (dresses in a lovely attire). In his final classification of songs this one comes under 'Puja: Ananda' (Devotion: Joy). The second Sikh *bhajan* which he translated and published in 1914 comes under general devotion and prayer. The original text is:

e Hari sundar e Hari sundar
tero charanpar sir naaveñ.
sevak janke seva seva par
premi janaañke prem prem par
duhki janaañke bedan bedan
sukhi janaañke aananda e.
banaa-banaameñ saañval saañval

giri-girimeñ unnita unnita
salitaa-salitaa cañcal cañcal
saagar-saagar gambhir e.
chandra suraj baroi niramal dipaa
tero jagamandir ujaar e.

The Bengali is very close, beginning exactly as the original ('e Hari sundar, e Hari sundar'), only the 'mastak nami taba charan-'pare' ('tero charanpar sir naaveñ') is added three additional times as the refrain. As to how these two Sikh *bhajans* reached Tagore, the first must have come from the famous Santiniketan medievalist Kshitimohan Sen's collection (whose Kabir he would soon use for his translations), even if his niece, Indira Devi might have acted as some kind of a catalyst. The path of the second one has not yet been traced. Did his other niece, elder sister's daughter, Sarala Devi who was in the Punjab by marriage, get it for him? For lack of evidence we can only conjecture. All we know is that its translation by Tagore was published in the periodical *Prabasi* in 1914 with the note that this 'aarati' had come from Amritsar's Gurudarbar.

If we take a look at the songs he was composing at the time of 'baaje baaje ramyabinaa baaje', we are struck by their closeness to it. Not that they are all of the same temper: there is variation on the joy or wonder, or that again is taken over by doubt or even anxiety. The song that immediately precedes it is:

Look, how beautifully this joyous evening is spread!
In a gentle breeze in the upper air
floats a melancholy and expectant sweetness.
In silenced skies the planets and stars

> quietly pour the nectar of light-rays' music.
> My heart and mind fill slowly up with relish,
> and body thrilled with unbound pleasure, look.

And the song that comes one song after is:

> From where rings this love's sensation!
> Is it my beloved friend stepping
> to my heart's darkened yard?
> Throw out all your pettiness, you,
> and wake up happy, Oh life.
> Light all your lamps, light all—
> and in an eager voice call, 'come my dearest'.

In other words, what I am saying is that the Sikh *bhajan*, as rewritten by Tagore, fits in with the songs he was writing at the time. And though the second *bhajan*, 'e Hari sundar e Hari sundar', has the temper of a *brahmasamgit*, it does not seem utterly out of place among the songs that precede and follow it. The one immediately preceding is non-ceremonial but not un-Nanak-like:

> It is for you and me to crown our love that light fills up the sky.
> It is for you and me to crown our love that the green earth
>   bursts into blooms.
> It is for you and me to crown our love
> that night wakes with the world in lap,
> and dawn comes to open the eastern door full of voices.
> The love-hope-boat has been floating on eternal streams.
> Endless time's flowers overflow their baskets.

It is for you and me to crown our love
that age after age in this universe
my heart goes in bride's dress self-seeking its consort.

But the one before two songs may keep our *bhajan* better company:

I shall sing your tune give me that *veena*,
I shall hear your words give me that undying spell.
I shall serve you give me that great strength,
I shall gaze at your face give me that firm devotion.
I shall bear your blows give me that immense patience,
I shall carry your flag give me that unflinching steadiness.
I shall claim all earth give me that roaring life,
I shall make myself pauper give me that love's gift.
I shall go with you give me that right hand,
I shall fight in your battle give me that weapon of yours,
I shall wake up in your truth give me that call.
I shall give up happiness' slavery give oh give me goodness.

Year 1909 to 1914, in fact somewhat earlier than 1909 to somewhat later than 1914, was a period in Tagore's career as a composer when the spirit of Nanak, and Kabir, and of a number of other Sants from medieval India seemed to have fit into his creative psyche. We recall that in 1914 he brought out, with assistance from Evelyn Underhill, *One Hundred Poems of Kabir*. Notwithstanding the scholarly doubt about the full authenticity of his Kabir sources, his regard for Kabir cannot be denied. But some of his western admirers' putting Kabir and him on the same scale and preferring Kabir to him was misjudgement, for Kabir was primarily a Sant whose poetry, oral, was only an effective medium. Tagore on the other hand was primarily a poet and composer (Sant Tagore would indeed be a travesty) fully conscious of his craft, though experiencing a degree of devotion in the period we are talking of. Obviously the same distinction applies to Guru Nanak and Tagore, Sant and poet. (Perhaps we would understand this distinction better if we place Tagore by someone nearer home, Ramakrishna whose words were as full of faith as wisdom and who by all means was a saint.) To Tagore Kabir and Nanak were true propagators of what he meant by *dharma*; and what he meant by it would perhaps be clear from the following excerpts from his essay, 'The Simple Ideals of Dharma' in 1903:

> If I have to light a lamp at home, I have to make much effort—I have to depend on so many people. I have to keep track of where mustard is sown, where oil is pressed from it, the whereabouts of the oil market, and then there is all the going about dressing up a lamp—after such elaborations what meagre light do I get? My immediate purpose may be served, but it only doubles the dense darkness outside.
>
> To get the world-revealing morning light I don't have to depend on anyone—don't have to manufacture it; all I have to do is wake up. As I open my eyes and unbar my door that light floods in which no one can stop.
>
> As this great light is, so is *dharma*. It too is immense, it too is simple. It is God gifting Himself—it is timeless, it is boundless; by surrounding us, by overlapping our inner and outer selves, it holds itself up. To have it, we

only need to ask for it, to open our hearts. As getting a sky-full of daylight by making an extra effort is not getting it, so finding our eternal life's refuge, *dharma* by making special arrangements would never materialise.

What we get to manufacture ourselves becomes complicated. Our society is complicated, our corporate life is complicated, and our everyday living is complicated. This complication, by its show of many-sided variety and by pretending to be big and mighty, often overpowers our confused self. Our unknowing mind ascribes great scholarship to the philosophical treatise that is most roundabout, and is struck with wonder. The civilisation whose processes are difficult and confusing, whose factories and arrangements cum materials are far-flung, overwhelms our unsophisticated mind. But the philosopher who can present philosophy in simple clarity is truly worthy and intelligent; the civilisation that can put its system in simple order and is in every way amenable is truly advanced. Whatever the outward look, complication as such is hollowness, proof of failure; fullness is simplicity. *Dharma* is the most perfect instance of that fullness, hence of simplicity.

Let me give an example. Home is necessary to us, our habitation. The open sky is not habitable to us like that. But to keep this open sky open is absolutely necessary to us. By maintaining an untrammelled link between the open sky and the spaces inside our home is how we can save our home from being our prison or our grave. But if we say, 'we shall make the sky our own like our home', if we keep raising walls into the

> sky, then our home alone has its extension, the open sky moves further and further away.

It is in the above perspective that we may now look up his essay 'Shivaji o Guru Gobindasingha' written in 1910 as the preface to Sarat Kumar Roy's (a teacher at his school at Santiniketan) book *SikhGuru o Sikh Jati*. Unlike his three earlier essays it was not addressed to juvenile readers; he was not instructing, he was trying to make a serious reflection on the Sikh Panth as moulded away from Guru Nanak's message of universal love. He opens by distinguishing Maratha history under Shivaji which was political, committed to setting up a Hindu kingdom throughout India. On the other hand, Sikh history at the outset was religious. 'The freedom that Baba Nanak had felt was not political freedom; his sense of *dharma* was not constricted by the worship of deities that was limited to a certain country's or people's imagination and habit and did not accommodate the universal human heart, on the contrary restrained it; his heart was free from the bonds of these narrow mythological religions and he dedicated his life to preaching that freedom to all.' 'But come to be oppressed by the Mughals the disciples of Nanak turned into a community of their own, and for that reason their prime effort became defending themselves from harassment and surviving, rather than preaching religion all around. Thus from outside pressure the Sikhs became a closely knit race. Their last Guru was especially devoted to this task. … It really was not a religious preacher's task; it was mainly an army general and politician's task. Guru Gobind had that quality. He was a warrior that could muster his followers with a singular determination and overpower the enemy. … Guru

Gobind wavered in keeping to the sense of freedom that Guru Nanak had taken to be greater than everything else.' This is the thrust of Tagore's argument. He sums it up in the following words. 'Nanak gave a call to his disciples to be free from selfishness, religious bigotry and spiritual inertia—he wanted their humanness to have a great success. Guru Gobind bound the Sikhs to a particular necessity, and so that they are never forgetful of it he imprinted it in their hearts by name, attire, ritual and several other means.' Tagore does take up Maharaja Ranjit Singh but as the very opposite of Guru Nanak, as a flaming comet that burned only for a while. He bemoans the outcome of Sikh history. Like a river it had issued from a snowy mountain top. But instead of making its way towards the ocean it goes meandering in the sand.

Tagore does make a difference between Guru Gobind and Shivaji's aims, but cannot ignore the eventual failure of Maratha history as well, the reasons not simply being Shivaji's incompetent successors but also Shivaji's own disregard of the leaks in Hindu society without mending which no salvage was possible. In conclusion he says: 'Anyway, by comparing the rise and fall of Marathas and Sikhs it can be said, that the Sikhs were once united by the call of a great thought—they had heard the message of a truth that was not confined to the perpetual practice at a certain place and did not rise from the excitement of a certain time—that belonged to all time and all men, that broadened the scope of both the small and the big, released the mind, and accepting which was for everyone to realise the fullest glory of humanness. Answering this call of Nanak's generous religion, the Sikhs through centuries grew up while bearing many hardships. By the glory of this religiosity and hardships the Sikhs had an invisible unity founded among them.' Guru Gobind reoriented this unity from thought to action and achieved a temporary goal, but at the cost of permanence.

We know that this reading of Sikh history did not go down well with intellectuals and historians, Sikh or non-Sikh, except for Jadunath Sarkar whose appreciation even made him publish an English translation of the piece in *The Modern Review* in 1911. But what is of more immediate interest is what caused Tagore's shift from his earlier admiration of Guru Gobind Singh. How did he wake up to the militant character of his *karma*, and to its limiting outcome? Or was he apprehensive of *karma* as such carried out at a national scale feeding on hatred? Yet as late as 1904 he had celebrated Shivaji in an encomium for the impending Shivaji Festival. His disillusion with *karma* bereft of *dharma* must have come from the excesses and the communally exclusive nature of the *Svadeshi* and Boycott movements keeping the Bengal Muslims at bay and causing Hindu-Muslim riots. He had initially been part of these movements but soon withdrew. The ground was getting ready for his first political novel *Ghare-Baire* (1916: *The Home and the World*) which would draw no less flak perhaps than the essay on Sikh history. It was a coincidence, yet perhaps no coincidence, that he would write his Nationalism lectures the same year in Japan that were not without any bearing on nationalism or nationalisms in India.

Jallianwala Bagh might have been anywhere in India and Tagore would have protested, but its being in Amritsar might have had a special association for him. Similarly, a friend reminds me, the second line of *janaganamana* to begin with Panjab ('Panjab Sindhu Gujarat Maratha Dravid Utkal Banga') may be suggestive of special affection. Yet the estrangement caused by the essay we just discussed went on for over two decades. Eventually during his visit to Lahore in early 1935 things cleared up: Tagore addressed the Fifth Punjab Students' Conference, read his poetry at the Y.M.C.A., and had a warm reception from the local Sikh leaders. On return he wrote a poem, his sixth 'Sikh' poem. It was included as Poem 33 in *Sesh Saptak* (Last Septet), a book of prose poems printed in 1935. The same year a slightly different version of the poem came out in the periodical *Prabasi* under the title 'Sikh'. Here is *Sesh Saptak* 33:

> Emperor's order—
> with forces came Afrasayeb Khan, Muzaffar Khan,
> Muhammad Amin Khan,
> and with them came King Gopal Singh Bhadauria,
> Udait Singh Bundela.
>
> The Mughal army laid a siege to Gurudaspur.
> The Sikhs were inside the fort,
> Banda Singh their leader.
> Supplies have been cut off,
> All outside exits shut.
> Cannon balls come pelting from time to time
> bounding over the walls,
> to the horizon on four sides
> the night sky is red with flaming torches.

No wheat is left in the stores, no rye,
no maize either;
the firewood too has exhausted.
In unbearable hunger they are eating raw meat,
some even eat slices cut from their own thighs.
Grounding barks and branches from trees,
they dough their bread.

Eight months passed in this hellish suffering,
then to Mughals fell
the Gurudaspur fort.
Death's court fills up to neck with blood,
the prisoners cry out
'Wahi Guru, Wahi Guru',
and Sikhs' heads keep rolling
day after day.

Boy Nehal Singh;
in his clear young and gentle face
blooms an inner light.
In his eyes seems held
the morning pilgrims' song.
A lissome bright body,
the divine sculptor has fashioned out
with lightning's chisel.
Age eighteen or nineteen.
a sal tree's sapling,
risen straight up,
can still sway in the southern breeze.
Life's abundance is

in body and mind
full to the brim.

He was brought in chains.
All court's eyes
gazed at his face in wonder and pity.
For an instant
the executioner's sword seemed reluctant.
At that moment a messenger came from the capital,
with the release-order in hand
signed by Syed Abdulla Khan.

When his hand-clasps were untied,
the boy asked, 'Why this special judgement to me?'
Was told, his widowed mother had informed—
her son was not Sikh by religion,
that, the Sikhs had by force
kept him captive.

In anger and shame went red
the boy's face.
He shouted out, 'I don't want life by a lie,
in truth is my final liberation,
I am Sikh.'

Is Nehal Singh grown up from Banda's infant son, a martyr in the making? And have I come full circle to 'Bandi Bir'?

2014

Tagore's Travel Writings

Taking travel writing to be a genre, we shall try to see how Tagore handles it. Travel is the tale of a *homo viator*, a man on the road. We shall try to see how that tale is told by Tagore. Travel writing is the traveller writing his/her own travel. It is a kind of partial autobiography. However, the traveller may have a companion who too may be writing down the travel. This is what happened in Bashō's northern journey in 1689, *Oku no Hosomichi* (The Narrow Road through the Provinces). He had Sora with him who kept a travel diary (*Nikki* [Diary Accompanying Bashō on the Narrow Road through the Provinces]). Similarly Samuel Johnson had his Scottish journey with James Boswell in 1773. And they both wrote down the travel, Johnson his *Journey* (*A Journey to the Western Islands of Scotland*) and Boswell his *Tour* (*The Journal of a Tour to the Hebrides with Samuel Johnson*). Earl Miner has done a thorough study of these two pairs, approaching them in terms of onomastics: *Naming Properties: Nominal Reference in Travel Writings by Bashō and Sora, Johnson and Boswell* (Ann Arbor: The University of Michigan Press, 1996).

Though Tagore had companions in almost all his travels, he does not have a regular Sora or Boswell. However, during his travel to Indonesia in 1927 one of his companions, Suniti Kumar Chatterji the linguist wrote a detailed account putting Tagore's *Javajatrir Patra* (Letters from Java) in perspective. Earlier in 1924, his travel to China and, a second time, to Japan had been recorded by a similar companion, the historian Kalidas Nag. Tagore had not written down that travel; so there is no paralleling.

His son Rathindranath's diaries and memoirs also supplement his own records of travel to England and America in 1912-13, to England, America and the Continental Europe in 1920-21, and to Italy on his way back from Argentina in 1925. His son at times might have been a Sora to his Bashō, giving us the missing facts.

Now, to go back to the generic question of Tagore's travel writings, let us approach them individually. The first is *Europe-prabasir Patra* (Letters from a Sojourner in Europe), the outcome of his first travel to England at seventeen in his elder brother Satyendranath's company and his sojourn there for about a year and a half. These 'Letters' are written home, to be published in *Bharati* edited by his eldest brother Dwijendranath. They contain his comments on English life and manners with a special focus on women. They also contain his critique of the newly arrived Bengalis aping the English. These 'Letters' are perhaps, no matter how distantly, of the same genre as Montesquieu's *Lettres persanes* or Voltaire's *Lettres philosophiques* or Lowes Dickinson's *John the Chinaman's Letters* which he would be reviewing in two decades.

His second piece of travel writing is *Europe-jatrir Diary* (Diary of a Traveller to Europe) covering his short second trip to and from England in 1890. He first made a draft of it; then rewrote it. In citing the nominal reference in Bashō-Sora and Johnson-Boswell's travels, Earl Miner focuses on the 'names' of places, persons and on time. Though the places and persons are not a few in *Europe-prabasir Patra*, the temporality of that travel cum sojourn is relatively sparse. The *Diary*, on the other hand, is written temporally, date by date. It begins with an entry on 'Friday. 22nd August 1890' and ends on one on '4 November'. In between, the calendar is only occasionally interrupted. One entry is double-dated, and on one date there are two entries. It may seem that he is both his Bashō and Sora.

His second visit to England had no plans for a sojourn. The third visit, in 1912-13, combined America with England. So did the fourth visit, in 1920-21, which also included a part of the Continental Europe. These two travels were written down as essays which are more reflective than informative.

But between these two western trips, he made his first eastern trip. To Japan in 1916, and it was in the wake of his Nobel fame. *Japan-jatri* (Traveller to Japan) has fifteen chapters. Of them, eleven are devoted to the way. After the familiar route of Aden to Suez to Alexandria/Port Said to Brindisi/Marseilles, we now have Rangoon (Yangon), Penang, Singapore, Hong Kong, Kobe—an altogether new world. The chapters flow into one another with an emphasis on 'seeing'. His 'seeing' takes on a special significance when at Hong Kong he observes Chinese dock labourers at work making him reflect on the strength of the Chinese people as a whole. The twelfth chapter deals with the arrival in Japan and the immediate aftermath. Tagore's impressions of Japan are carried in the three remaining chapters.

His next travelogue is *Pashcim-jatrir Diary* (Diary of a Westward Traveller), dated 1924-25. It covers his Peru-bound trip to South America which terminated in Argentina, and return from there. Though it is called a *Diary*, it is not one like *Europe-jatrir Diary*. The entries do have a date suggesting a passage of time, but there is hardly any mention of place. His passage back from Argentina is not included (in the *Diary* there is an abrupt changeover from the onward boat 'Haruna-Maru' to the return boat 'Cracovia'). We learn from his son's diaries of his arrival at Genoa on 15 January.

Javajatrir Patra comes next, covering his visit to Indonesia and Siam (Thailand) in 1927, chiefly to Bali and Java. However, in 1926 he had gone to Europe again, but did not write down that travel except for his journey back including a visit to Egypt in a few letters to Rani Mahalanobis. Similarly in a couple of letters he will tell her of his journey in 1929 to Canada via China (touching only Shanghai) and Japan—no travelogue at all. Further, in another batch he is going to tell her of his trip to Europe in 1930, the focus being on the appreciation of his paintings. There is also a mention of his trip to America on that occasion.

But the Java letters, written to several persons including Rani or Nirmalkumari Mahalanobis, amount to a full-fledged travelogue. The others to whom they are addressed are his daughter-in-law Pratima Devi, literary secretary Amiya Chakravarty, son Rathindranath and daughter Mira Devi. In all it is twenty-one letters, two of which have an unnamed addressee. They are spanned from mid-July to October-beginning.

The travelogue that comes next is *Russiar Chithi* (Letters from Russia), outcome of his visit to Soviet Russia in 1930. The number of letters is fifteen, three of which are written from Moscow, three from Berlin on return from Moscow, seven from 'SS Bremen', one from Lansdowne, USA, and a concluding letter. They have been written respectively to Rathindranath, Nirmalkumari Mahalanobis, Prasantachandra Mahalanobis, Asa Adhikari, Surendranath Kar, Ramananda Chattopadhyay, Nandalal Bose, Kalimohan Ghosh and Sudhindranath Datta. Their time-span is 19 September to 28 October. The text of *Russiar Cithi* has three appendices: "Grambasidiger Prati" (To the Villagers), "Palliseva" (Village Service) and "Koreo Jubaker Rashtrik Mat" (Political Views of a Korean Youth). The third one is of particular relevance to the *Letters*: there is a reference to his conversation with this Korean youth in Tokyo in *Letter* 3. Tagore must have met him in 1929, probably on his sudden return to Japan from America after the unpleasantness at the U.S. immigration. He readily set out to write down their conversation, but ended up writing a piece on 'Dhyani Japan' (Meditative Japan). In fact, it begins by saying that he had been invited to Korea from where he had thought of going overland to Russia. But his health did not even permit him to go to Korea.

Tagore's last travelogue is *Parasye* (In Persia) covering his visit to Iran and Iraq in 1932. This is neither a diary nor a batch of letters, nor individual essays strung together; it is straight narration—of course in the first person. There are eleven chapters in it depicting the different phases of his journey cum visit. First the flight, for he flew to Iran stopping at Allahabad, Jodhpur, Karachi, Jāsk and then the destination Būshehr. This was the second time he was flying—the first time had been from London to Paris—and he did not like it. He preferred sailing or taking the train. The train he will have at the Iraq border, but in Iran all his travelling is done by road. From Būshehr to Shīrāz is his first haul. At Shīrāz he visits Sa'di and Ḥāfez's graves. At Ḥāfez's grave he performs the local ritual of opening the poet's *Divan* at random with closed eyes and a question in mind. And he seems to have an answer. On his way from Shīrāz to Eṣfahān he sees the ruins of Persepolis. From Eṣfahān he goes to Tehrān. What strikes him in Iran is her modernisation under Reza Shah Pahlavi. He meets him and is impressed by his unassuming mien and dedication. He will have a similar impression of Iraq's Faisal who too is an emblem of new Asia—first manifest in the region in Turkey's Kemalpasha.

Tagore's birthday falling during his Iran visit and his hosts celebrating it, he writes a poem on Iran. From Tehrān he travels to Iraq and arrives at Bagdad by train. What he marks most in Faisal's Iraq, as he has also done in Reza Shah's Iran, is religious tolerance, missing in his own country at the moment. The last leg of his visit is to a Bedouin tent in the Arab desert. The Bedouin chief quoting the Prophet's saying that a true Muslim is he whose words and actions do not hurt anyone, leaves a lasting impression on Tagore's mind.

It turns out then that Tagore's travel writings are of different kinds. We have letters that go commenting at the first opportunity; again letters that touch upon a travel in passing. In between we have letters that tell a travel in detail. We have a diary that mainly quotes events date by date; and again a diary that goes on a given date reflecting. We have narrations. Finally, we have isolated pieces that add up to a travel.

Western travel was not uncommon to Indians in the late 19th century when Tagore first sailed to England. But eastern travel was, though his father had visited China. It is not that he was following his father's footsteps, but came to develop his own interest in China and Japan. In 1902 he met Okakura at Jorasanko which facilitated a relationship with the land of the rising sun. Of course the Nobel Prize came in handy by making him the pride of Asia. Japan had a 'Tagore boom' and China a 'Tagore fever'. However, his interest in China goes back early when he wrote against Britain's opium trade there. As noted above and will also be noted below, he reviewed *John the Chinaman's Letters* too, where he marked India's affinity with China. So, his eastern travel is in one way his encounter with the larger Asia. In fact his travel later to Iran and Iraq falls in line with those to China and Japan.

But this does not propose an either-or. In spite of Europe's marauding of Asia, Europe needs her as much as Asia needs Europe. In Chapter 2 of *Parasye* he develops this idea. 'When I was young I had a great relish in reading European literature and had a great regard for the European man of science. … I remember in Iraq a respectable gentleman asked me, "What is your view of the English people?" I said, 'The best of them are the best of the human race.' With a smile he said, 'And those that are the next best?' I was quiet. … In Asia we have most of our business with these next best. … Probably on the European stage the scene is shifting to the fifth act. And the signs of an Asian renaissance are spreading from one horizon to another. … I believe if Asia cannot fully wake, Europe has no rescue.'

These words bear the tenor of much of Tagore's travel writings, particularly since World War I which hurt him deeply. The War was greed galore and science was made to play the role of its henchman. He admired Japan's awakening, but at the same time cautioned her against nationalist excesses. That may explain his emphasis on what constitutes the characteristic Japanese qualities of the Japanese people. He says somewhere that Okakura had asked him to visit China to appreciate the spirit of East Asia. He did visit China though he did not write down that travel. But the talks he gave there were witness to his travel thoughts, pleading with China not to forget her millennial past nor set up a purely industrial future.

The thrust of *Javajatrir Patra* is on yet another piece of Asia which had once come under Indian influence but has since developed on her own. Though Java is Muslim and Bali Hindu, their culture is on the whole the same. They cherish the same myths from the *Rāmāyaṇa* and *Mahābhārata* in a pristine form. But what is most amazing is their dance, as if it were their natural language. Tagore's letters are full of dances he saw. In one letter he uses a metaphor to characterise this dance: It is 'not like the patter of pouring rains, but like the flow of a wavy stream.' (Letter 11) In another (14) he says: 'Carried away by loss and gain, by pleasure and pain, human life is ever at play with form, with sound and touch; if all that is to be expressed in sound alone, it becomes splendorous music; likewise, if leaving all else it is to be expressed in movement alone, it turns into dance.'

At Borobudur he deplored the tourists' vacant gaze and wrote a poem that ends on:

> It is time that
> man sick and bound,
> came to this holy place
> again
> to read
> the words carved on the silent stone—
> that, piercing a thousand years' ruckus,
> ring out in the skies forever,
> words of eternal love, 'Buddhaṁ śaraṇaṁ gacchāmi'.
> ('Borobudur,' *Parisesh*)

Tagore could not visit Korea, but his conversation with the Korean youth may be taken as a surrogate visit. The moot part of that text is:

> … the epoch making conflict that has begun today in the world is not between the different races, but between the two parts of humanity, the ruler and the ruled, the oppressor and the oppressed. Here the Korean and the Japanese, the eastern and the western are in the same boat. Our sufferings, our destitution are our strength. … On the contrary, those that are rich cannot be united; they are separated by the impassable wall of self-interest. …

Tagore mused over the Korean youth's tenets of class struggle. He was not sure if some difference was not necessary. Besides, the class struggle means violence. And that will lead to a cycle of bloodshed. This was before his visit to Soviet Russia which would modify his views and give a new meaning to his conversation with the Korean youth.

❧

Perhaps of all Tagore's writings depicting his western travel, *Russiar Chithi* has had the widest reception. The keyword in these 'Letters' is wonder—wonder at what Soviet Russia has achieved in mass education and social equality in so short a time, and with such hostility around. The wonder is also at the Soviet leap in agriculture, especially through cooperative farming. He does not seem tired of his encomium because throughout he is haunted by a contrast with his own country. But there is a doubt lurking as to the dictatorial hand behind the Soviet achievement. True, the wretched of the earth have been given human dignity, but has that involved a sacrifice of their individuality? Yet I wonder if he would have approved if he were still alive, Louis Fischer, André Gide, Arthur Koestler, Ignazio Silone, Stephen Spender and Richard Wright's invective, *The God that Failed.*

He was seventy when he came to Russia and seventeen when he had first gone to England. His first impression of England is worth quoting:

> Before coming to England I had expected … that this tiny island of two cubits' breadth is everywhere resounding with Gladstone's oratory, Max Mueller's Vedic interpretations, Tyndall's scientific theories, Carlyle's profound thoughts, Benn's philosophical treatises. Fortunately I have been disappointed. (Letter 2)

Though green, there was perhaps no lack of self-confidence in the seventeen year-old Tagore's comments on English life. We may contrast this with Gandhi's first year in England at the age of eighteen, so unsure and yet so resolute. Of course their circumstances were different: Tagore had his family's indulgence; Gandhi was on his own but morally bound to his family.

There is no doubt that Tagore liked sea travels. It gave him ample opportunity to reflect, and some of his reflections on board are among his best non-fiction prose. *Pashcim-jatrir Diary* is an instance of how the mind picks up one thread of thought after another. At one point it focuses on woman's nature as opposed to that of man. Man ever thrusts, woman holds: they are complementary. *Pashcim-jatrir Diary* is particularly supple in its 'Cracovia' portion: it is consciousness at a veritable flow. However, two of his favourite gleanings from the Upanishsads do come up there: *mā gṛdha* and *apāvṛṇu*. He takes the British fleecing of India to be a manifestation of greed. And all true art to him, in fact all true perception, is a tryst to the truth.

He also sees greed behind industrial pollution. In *Japan-jatri* his first encounter with Rangoon on the banks of Iravati repulses him:

> When the factory became the bearer of commerce, commerce lost its good looks. This will be clearly seen if we compare ancient Venice with modern Manchester. In Venice through her beauty and wealth man left his own imprint, in Manchester man has dwarfed himself in every respect and gave imprint to his factories. (Ch. 4)

With Japan it was not just industrialisation but her amazing westernisation. For 'in Asia it was Japan that suddenly one day felt, that Europe could only be resisted by the power through which she had won over everyone.' (Ch. 15)

When in 1927 he comes to Bali and Java he has a surprise waiting for him. They are almost idyllic. He has wonder of course, but joy too to witness a people which have kept up so much India had once brought them, but a people since distanced. Indeed as an epistolary travelogue *Javajatrir Patra* is no less than *Russiar Chithi*, even though the latter is historically more important.

We recall Tagore at Ḥāfez's grave from *Parasye*. The wish he had framed to be fulfilled by Ḥāfez's *Divan* was: 'Let India be freed of the mortal noose of religious blindness.' Sitting by Ḥāfez's grave he felt an affinity with him:

> … my mind was suddenly stirred up, in the sunshine of this spring morning the poet's smiling eyes sent me an intimation from a distant spring day. It seemed we two were friends in the same drinking inn and had many times filled up many cups with various juices. I too have often been subjected to the religious zealots' crooked brow. Their rhetorical mesh could not bind me; a run-away I have taken a holiday in the free-flowing breeze of joy. I am certain, after hundreds of years, crossing the bar of many lives and deaths, a mendicant has come to this graveside today who is ever known to Ḥāfez. (Ch. 4) (Incidentally, Ḥāfez was Rabindranath's father Debendranath's favourite poet.)

Travel writing is the record of the traveller's 'self' encountering the travelled to land's 'other'. How much is the 'self' possessed by the 'other'? Or is the 'other' largely an extension of the 'self'? Absolute possession will amount to topography. Absolute extension will amount to egoism.

We may stretch this to the encounter of one culture with another. If relativism applies to the visited culture, relativism also applies to the visiting culture. But it does not amount to a clash but a meeting. Ideally a dialogue takes place, though with room for misunderstanding. The business of the true traveller is to have wonder. A cliché may be in order: not all are travellers, only some are.

There is an added dimension to Tagore's travels, his world-consciousness. He is not merely visiting another country, but reaching the world through her. Of the many complementarities in him is *svadesh* and *visva*—and, not versus. There is no home to him without his world, and there is no world to him without his home. In many ways is he Goethe's peer, in this combination too; but while Goethe might have been hinting at a distance between *Nationalliteratur* and *Weltliteratur* Tagore's *Visvasahitya* includes a whole host of *svadeshi sahitya*.

Let me end with Annadasankar Ray's clerihew on Tagore the traveller:

> Rabindranath Tagore
> is now going to Pakurh.[1]

1 Pakurh is only a few hours' journey from Santiniketan.

Not to China or Peru either,
Doesn't generosity lie there?

(Rabindranath Thakur
ebar jacchen Pakurh.
China, kimba Peru na,
seikhanei to karuna.)

Presented at the Fourth International Congress of Bengal Studies at the Tokyo University of Foreign Studies, 2015

Tagore's Vision of the East

(May I propose a disclaimer? Vision is a loaded word. Not only not everyone has a vision, but also those who have one may not always have the same contours to it. On that count the visionary in question may draw some flak from some quarters. On the other hand, those who follow his lead may go on justifying him. This may particulary be the case of an extraordinary creative man like Rabindranath Tagore. He may have a vision now and then, but he does not do his creative act in order to illustrate that vision; on the contrary the vision may be an inference thereof. A biography some time ago has donned him the Shakespearean epithet, 'myriad-minded'. He is indeed myriad-minded, not simply because of his infinite generic variety—how many of his time have been such makers of words in all their possible forms, yet written music and painted and done theatre and choreography?—but also because of his infinite love of man and nature. A mind ever on the move, he is like a river; taking turns here and there while adding verdure to the shores, to be never

dammed up to benefit some and deprive many. There is no dearth of thought in him, but to call him a thinker is a kind of myopia that denies him his full. Being often caught between the Rabindranath and the Tagore of his name, he needs must be defended from that myopia. So I shall ask my reader to take the word 'Vision' of my title tentatively, in lieu of something better.)

'Look East' has been a slogan for some time. Whether it survives or not, it takes us back to Tagore who told us to look east over a hundred years ago. Since 1901 he had been thinking of seeing Japan. In 1902 he met Okakura of the Japan Art Institute fame at his family home in Kolkata—Okakura who believed in Asian unity. And it was Okakura who had given him, that very year, his first international student at Santiniketan, the young ardent Buddhist Shitoku Hori. (Hori's journal had a record of Tagore's request to help him trace the Sanskrit Buddhist texts long transported to China and Japan.) Again it was Okakura who had sent his close associates in the new art movement, Taikan Yokoyama and Shunso Hishida, in 1903 to meet him. Through Okakura he had also got his Jujutsu teacher for Santiniketan, Jinnotsuke Sano, in 1905. The same year he wrote an article, 'Japaner Prati' (To Japan), for the magazine *Bhandar* (Treasure) congratulating Japan on her victory over Russia and invoking in a Japanesse-style poem if India that had given Japan *dhyana* might not now imbibe *karma* from her. 1905 being the year of agitation over the proposed Bengal Partition, this invocation had an added meaning. In 1911 he met the Buddhist scholar Ryukan Kimura in Kolkata who went to Japan at his request in 1915 to fix his probable itinerary. That visit we know did not come through and it was only the year after that he went to Japan on his way to America.

Even these bare details would show how close he felt to Japan. He did not feel any less close to China though the visit did not take place before 1924. In fact his awareness dates earlier. In 1881 he had published an impassioned essay against the opium trade perpetrated in China by Britain, 'Chine Maraner Byabasay' (Death Trade in China) in the magazine *Bharati* (Writings) in its May issue. In an essay in 1901 on the difference between societies ('Samajbhed') his immediate concern was the European barbarism in China for the resistance offered to the Christian missionaries' assault on the native practices, in which he spoke not for China alone but India as well, or for Asia as a whole. Another essay came out the year after, titled 'Chinemyaaner Chithi' (Chinaman's Letters), citing a newly printed booklet in English comprising a supposed[1] Chinese expatriate's critique of English customs in the light of the Chinese. Again the thrust is on Asia:

> This little book has given us as much happiness as strength. It has shown that there is a deep and wide-ranging unity among the various Asian peoples. On seeing India's inner affinity with China, our heart gladdens. Not that alone; the book also tells us of the wrong in Asia's being ever a defendant in Europe's court and ever taking her verdict as the last word, admitting that our only good lies in rooting out the three-fourths of our society along with their very foundation, and in

1 It was actually an Englishman, as Tagore found out later, by the name of Galsworthy Lowes Dickinson.

> replacing them with the English brick and mortar as planned out by the English engineers; and [the book] tells us of the need for putting Europe too in our court arraigning her for many of her extremely serious flaws.

I could go on and show that there was not so much an essentialist argument here of Asia versus Europe, East versus West, as an argument arising out of the historical contingency of Asia being dominated and browbeaten by Europe. For first of all, he was writing for a Bengali (by extension an Indian) audience. Secondly he was writing at a crucial moment of colonial history. Could it not be an appeal to 'selfhood' in the face of the mighty 'other'? Another quotation may come in handy: 'The harder turns our conflict with the foreigner, the greater grows our eagerness to understand and attain ourselves. We can see that this is not our case alone. The conflict with Europe is waking up all civilised Asia. Asia today is set to realising herself consciously and hence with vigour. She has understood, *ātmānaṁ viddhi*, know thyself—that is the road to freedom. *Paradharmo bhayāvahaḥ*, in imitating others is destruction.'

This was in 1902, the same year as Tagore began his friendship with Japan. Surely he had come to know by then of Japan's new awakening, though its excesses he was yet to see. In an essay in 1904 ('Svadeshi Samaj') on native Indian society and its tradition of crisis management away from the European statist measures thrust upon it, he mentioned Japan's soldiers who were not cogs in an inhuman war machine but held by *dharma* to their emperor and land, thus being led if necessary to suicide. Incidentally, a debate recently cropped up in a certain section of Kolkata intellectuals on Tagore's idea of 'nation' as opposed to his idea of 'svadesh' or 'samaj', broadly his notion of 'atmashakti' or self-reliance, its clarity or contradictions, and its relevance or lack of relevance to our time. I am not here to judge its tenor, let alone clinch it, though I would not like to think that his thoughts are passé. Besides by his vision of the East, I am mainly thinking of his love of Asia. Also, that love does not mean that he was hostile to the West. On the contrary, he valued West for a great many things we owed her. Indeed he was the last person to accept Kipling's famous/infamous statement 'never the twain shall meet'. One of the ironies of his life was that while he had been often taken as an apostle of the East abroad, at home he was often again taken for a votary of the West. And at home he could not keep company with the nationalists for long, though his concern for *svadesh* was no less than theirs. As such he was wary of nationalism, of the western variety in particular, for he knew it to be the breeding ground of colonialism. No wonder his book on *Nationalism* (1917), outcome of his Japan trip in 1916, would make its way into Lenin's reading list on India.

It is on record now that in spite of his admiration for the Asian roots of Japanese culture, and of Japan's admiration for the first Asian Nobel Laureate in literature, that trip went a little sour. The reason might have been more than one, though not excluding the words of caution he uttered against Japan's over-mechanisation and excessive emphasis on material culture. One might wonder if it was to Okakura's Japan he had gone or also in part to Count Ookuma's who wielded a lot of power and might have been an emblem of the expansionist ambition taking root in Japan's national psyche. It is also on record that while his arrival in Tokyo in 1916 fetched a big crowd, his arrival on his way back from America in 1917 at Yokohama was greeted by only a few! Yet Tagore would not lose his faith in Japan—he would come again in 1924 after his trip to China, and twice again in 1929, first Canada-bound and second, on his way back to soothe his nerves after the harassment at the U. S. immigration on the west coast (we recall that after arriving at San Francisco he instantly cancelled his appointments in the U.S.A.). Besides, his doors were ever open at Santiniketan to Japanese students and scholars. He too had left many marks in the land of the rising sun. Who would forget his description of Tanzan Shimomura's enormous painting 'Yoro-Boshi' (The Blind Man's Worship of the Sun) of which Kampo Arai made a copy for Him?

> Spring has come after winter; not a single leaf on plum branches, only some white flowers with petals falling off; at one end of the huge curtain the blood-red sun has appeared on the horizon, at the other end behind the bare plum branches a blind man with folded palms is worshipping the sun. A blind man, a tree, a sun and a gold-plated enormous sky; such painting I have never seen before. It was as if those words of prayer from the Upanishad have taken a shape for me—tamaso mā jyotirgamaya. Not the blind man's alone, blind nature's too was this prayer, tamaso mā jyotirgamaya—rising through the plum tree's devotion-stretched branches to the realm of light. (*Japan-Jatri* [Traveller to Japan], Ch. 14)

This art, he felt, was Japanese to the core, yet not revivalist, and obviously not European imitation. Arai also made a copy for him of a painting by Taikan; and here is the description: 'No excess, nor fashion. There was power in it and restraint. The theme is—a Chinese poet from the old is walking in an absolute trance; behind him a young boy is carrying with great care a lyre that has no strings; behind the boy is a bent willow.' (Ibid.) Again it was Tagore who first told us of the restraint of the Haiku: 'Old pond / a frog's leap / splash of water' (English rendering from his Bengali translation—now a classic to Bengali readers) (*ed. cit.*, Ch. 13). The Japan-India friendship that has built up over the last hundred years or so is in a way his dream come true—'yatra viśva bhavatyekanīdam' (Visva-Bharati's motto meaning 'where the world is one nest').

But by no means would he compromise on what he had said about Japan's drift towards nationalism. The two letters he wrote in 1938 in answer to his friend, poet Yone Noguchi's justifying Japan's war on China in the name of 'Asia for Asia' are proof thereof. 'The doctrine of "Asia for Asia" which you enunciate in your letter, as an instrument of political blackmail, has all the virtues of the lesser Europe which I repudiate and nothing of the larger humanity that makes us one across the barriers of political labels and divisions. I was amused to read the recent statement of a Tokyo politician that the military alliance of Japan with Italy and Germany was made for "highly spiritual and moral reasons" and "had no materialistic considerations behind them". Quite so. What is not amusing is that artists and thinkers should echo such remarkable sentiments that translate military swagger into spiritual bravado.' And he ended the second letter 'wishing your people whom I love, not success, but remorse.'[2] Tagore did not outlive the War, but he would have been the first to condemn Hiroshima, not take it as retribution. He would have wept with Japan.

In December 1939 Tagore welcomed the famous Chinese painter Xu Beihong (Ju Peon) to Santiniketan saying, 'With great joy I look forward to an era of warm kinship between our neighbouring lands and to the assertion of historical forces in the East that will save us from all encroaching darkness.'[3] That these words were deeply felt would soon be borne out by the words dictated on the occasion of his last birthday—words begun on a note of despair for the West's or England's breach of trust to civilisation leading to an utter crisis (as we know, the title of the text was 'Crisis in Civilization'), and ending on a note of hope: '... I shall not commit the grievous sin of losing faith in Man. I would rather look forward to the opening of a new chapter in his history after the cataclysm is over and the atmosphere rendered clean with the spirit of service and sacrifice. Perhaps that dawn will come from this horizon, from the East where the sun rises.'[4] I am not sure if the skeptics who would take him for a Pan-Asianist prophet, and a prophet manqué at that, have read this text carefully, or for that matter, his *Nationalism* essays or the talks he had given in China in 1924. There is also an interesting dialogue he had, as said above, with a Korean youth appended to *Russiar Chithi*, 1931 in which China is mentioned in a light that would demystify

2 *The English Writings of Rabindranath Tagore*, Vol. 3, ed. Sisir Kumar Das (New Delhi: Sahitya Akademi, 1996, rpt. 2002), pp. 837, 845.

3 *Ed. cit.*, p. 850.

4 Ibid. p. 726.

the prophet thesis. It is Tagore who is telling his interlocutor how necessary education is for a people:

> Look, there is China in front of you. True national self-respect hasn't awakened among the masses in that country for want of a proper education. So what we see there is an eddy of violence and strife among the greedy warlords grabbing at power. The unfortunate country is battered and wounded in aggressions and loot at the hands of marauders and musketeers, is covered with blood, and terrified in helpless fear. How are you going to fight such oppression of people by inner or outer aggressors unless people themselves come to realise their rights by education?

With these words and his earlier concern with China's plight, the opium war and the white man's 'yellow' peril, it should be obvious that he could not be preaching any essentialism in China during his visit in 1924, a blanket message that China should turn her back to the modern world. But she must not imitate the West as Japan in part was doing. He understood and tried his audience to understand that there was something precious in China's tradition. By no means was he a cultural relativist who only believed in China's Chinaness: how many of his time were as open as he was to the outside world that comprised a great deal of the globe? In fact he had a bad name for cosmopolitanism, better perhaps internationalism. The same year he visited China, and also Japan the second time, he went to Argentina. And that in a few years he would visit Soviet Russia was going to be glad news to the world left, let alone his detractors in China who took him for an oddity in 1924. All this is archive now, and the archivist is still arguing as to how 'controversial' a guest he really was. Was he at all, or was it a mere misapprehension on the part of the post-May Fourth modernists? For there is no denying that he left an impact, more perhaps than in many other countries. There is also no denying that he was not lecturing China but came with an offer of friendship from India. True he spoke against crass materialism, but not without praise for China's ethical regard over ages for material existence that has never been inhospitable to others. His target was self-centred commercialism, the kind he saw in Shanghai, the kind that existed in his native Calcutta under the British yolk. When Okakura had told him in 1913 to see China, he was probably thinking of the Buddhist roots of East Asian culture as well as China's immense possibilities as a great tradition.[5] And in 1924 Tagore's China on the one hand was India's China from a thousand years ago, her sister across the Himalayas, and fellow sufferer in the recent past, and on the other the China that is sure to surge forward with her youth on the vanguard. More often than not his talks were directed at them. His poetry too, that is, his own English translations of his Bengali poetry, had a double effect—on the one hand, we are told, his free verse was conducive to the new Chinese poetry that was trying to break away from strict rules; on the other hand its Chinese translation often added a stress on the spirit, as if to make up for its relative lack among the youth. Nonetheless it made a great impact, reportedly, one of the longest during in the world. His baptism by his hosts as 'Zhu

5 See Rabindranath Tagore, 'On Oriental Culture and Japan's Mission,' in *The English Writings of Rabindranath Tagore*, Vol. 3, *ed. cit.*, p. 605.

Zhendan' (India's Sun) on his 63rd (64th by the Chinese count) birthday was more than a mere decoration.

Yet there was apprehension, and among those who voiced that apprehension was Guo Moruo, a genuine admirer of his poetry and of the historic role he had been playing in India. Was the apprehension partly due to his immediate hosts whom the post-May Fourth modernists did not fully approve of at that critical juncture, especially, Liang Qichao, Hu Shi and Xu Zhimo? Yet it is on record that when he was leaving China at the end of that trip and was asked if any of his belongings had been left behind, he said that it was only a portion of his heart that he was leaving behind. That portion he would never call back, on the contrary let it thrive. That he did so is proved, among other things, by the warm friendship he developed with Xu Zhimo, warm enough to vie with his other international friendships. Not only did he give him a Bengali name, 'Susima', but paid him two short personal visits later (the earlier of which also left Xu Zhimo with a haunting four-line Tagore poem gifted by one of Tagore's travel companions, the young Bengali poet Sudhindranath Datta). Another remnant as it were of the Tagore heart in China, not less if not more, indeed much more, than Xu Zhimo (whose untimely death in an air crash cut short the future of his Tagore-*yana*), was Tan Yun-shan. It was on Tagore's invitation that he would come to Santiniketan in 1928 and form a Sino-Indian Cultural Society, first at Nanjing (1933), then at Santiniketan in 1934 leading to the famous 'Cheena-Bhavana' (China Hall) in 1937, and devote the rest of his life teaching and revealing China to Indians and imbibing India in his and his children's Chinese hearts, the 'Chindian' (Jairam Ramesh's coinage) spirit come to life.

And how deeply would Tagore feel for China during the Japanese aggression was not only borne by his letters to Noguchi but also by the words he sent to Chiang Kaishek in 1938 and 1939: 'China is great. Every day you are proving it at the cost of an incredible suffering and sacrifice. The heroism your people are displaying is epic in quality. I feel sure whatever may happen your victory will ever remain resplendent in the moral field of human endeavour.'[6] (This might remind us of what he had felt in 1916 on his way to Japan while watching the Chinese dock-workers unloading merchandise at Hong Kong: 'On seeing the power, the dexterity and joy of work in such harmony I realised what enormous energy had been storing all over the country among this great people. Here man has been long preparing for full application of himself. … When such energy will get the benefits of modern times, that is, master science, what power in the world can stop it?')[7]

Tagore did not pose as a prophet in China, nor earlier in Japan. The question would not arise in Indonesia or Thailand that he would be visiting in three years (1927). What he would be doing there was discover the Indian culture that had come there centuries ago and remained as it were in that pristine form. At the same time he would be taking a close look at what had developed there indigenously. His discovery of the Balinese dance would be no less momentous, for instance, than Antonin Artaud's, whose *Théâtre et son Double* made a mark in European theatre. But what distinguishes him from any European ecstasy (beyond of course the learned interest and study) is in the quality of that response devoid of any

6 *The English Writings of Rabindranath Tagore*, Vol. 3, *ed. cit.*, p. 832.

7 *Japan-Jatri*, Ch. 11.

'othering'. Indeed there had been no 'othering' with China and Japan as well, no matter how deeply he understood their respective uniqueness of culture. China he had valued as the oldest existing civilisation, Japan younger no doubt yet with a keen bearing of her essence—though fully aware of Buddha's *yana* in both.

Yet there is no denying that he felt strongly about Asia, that he had a feeling for the East. But his East was not the West's 'other'. His East was West's sister, perhaps the elder one. This in a way is borne out by two recent discoveries. Scientists have located South-east Turkey and the West Asian 'fertile crescent' as the area where man's eventual change from food-gatherer to food-producer began around 8000 BCE. Again archaeologists have discovered a set of six 'complete', 'multi-note' flutes as the 'oldest playable musical instruments' at an early Neolithic site called Jiahu dating back to 7000 BCE in China's Central Yellow River Valley between rivers Li and Sha. Don't these two locations add up to the surmise that perhaps 'civilisation' had been born nearer home, unless of course newer discoveries topple that, for what, after all, we call civilisation might not have had any fixed borders? The Jiahu flutes had been predated by the Ulm flute, whether of *Homo Sapien* or Neanderthal origin, and the Ulm flute by sure Neanderthal flute-like tools.[8] Fresh agricultural research seems to be on an older and more varied Neolithic track.

Obviously Tagore's feeling for the East had a special point in the context of colonialism and of the West's browbeating

8 See D. Balasubramanian, 'The Biology of Music: "Sobhillu Saptaswara",' in *Science*, *Literature* and *Aesthetics*, PHISPC, XV.3, ed. Amiya Dev (New Delhi: Centre for Studies in Civilizations, 2009), pp. 173-174

of Asia on many a count, especially for lagging behind on the path to progress. Asia's unconditional espousal of materialism at the expense of spirit was not the answer, for that would not give Asia back her self; on the contrary gradually erase it. True modern Europe had a lot to give and Asia had a lot to take, but for outer good Asia must not sacrifice her inner wealth. 'She alone can take who can give, the beggar cannot.'[9] But was it not ironical that what the colonial West kept taking from a large part of Asia was her *outer* wealth, indeed kept fleecing her turning the supposed beneficiaries into beggars? Tagore had been hoping against hopes—and he had reason for he had come across a number of large-hearted westerners—that human values would prevail and the West would not betray. But disillusion finally came with the War, and in the 'Crisis in Civilization' he recorded it pinning hope on the East. At the end of the Bengali text he has a song that is worth the humming: '*ai mahaamaanab aase*':

> There, the Saviour comes,
> the earth's dust and grass are all around
> stirred up.
> In heaven hail conches,
> victory drums on earth roll—
> the moment of the great birth is come.
> Night's fortress-towers are all
> tumbled to dust.
> On east's crest comes the call to cast out fear
> in hope of new life.
> 'All hail to human awakening'
> is ringing out in skies.

9 *Japane-Parasye* (in Japan and Persia), in *RR*, Vol. 12, *ed. cit*., p. 458.

Are we going to say, with World War turned memory, Hiroshima a reminder that there be not another world war, and colonialism consigned to archive, that we have made it in Asia? I would not conjure up Tagore's spirit to ask if this Asia is what he had in mind on his last birthday. But I would ask ourselves of the character of the strides we are taking today—are they or are they not a variation on the strides taken yesterday by the West? Is it or is it not the same grand narrative latent to our ideals of progress? Asia are we, but are not also part North and part South, though the configuration may be changing? Pardon my polemical tone, but the indices are not very happy. Global capital does not have any ethical compunction and most of us have as yet an enormous external debt. And it is not hard to say if our cultures too are not going to be swayed by that capital. Suppose we ask the Tagores of today to fetch their vision of tomorrow's Asia: what are we going to get? Asia or the West's double? Perhaps I am too overpowered by Tagore to allow the new Tagores a new vision. Or perhaps I am given to despair. Surely I would like nothing better than being proved wrong.

2011 (however a shorter version was presented at a joint conference at Jamia-Millia Islamia and Delhi University in 2006 on China, Japan and India): in Tagore and China, *eds. Tan Chung, Amiya Dev, Wang Bangwei, Wei Liming, ed. cit.*

Note on the Transliteration

For book and other titles in Bengali as well as for names, familiar renderings have been used—for instance, *Char Adhyay* and not *Caar Adhyaay*, *Raja* and not *Raajaa*; 'Sudarshana' and not 'Sudarsanaa', 'Bipradas' and not 'Bipradaas'. In quotations, a distinction has been made between 'a' (অ) and 'aa' (আ); 'ch' (চ) and 'chh' (ছ); 's'(স), 's' (শ) and 'sh' (ষ); and 'r' (র, ড়). However, 't' has been used for both 'ত' and 'ট'and 'd' for both 'দ', and 'ড', showing that the transliteration is more orthographic than phonetic.

Diacritics have been used in the Sanskrit quotations.